Steck-Vaughn

TABE FUNDAMENTALS

Focus on Skills

LEVEL D Applied Math

Reviewers

Victor Gathers
Regional Coordinator of Adult Services
New York City Department of Education
Brooklyn Adult Learning Center
Brooklyn, New York

Brannon Lentz
Assistant Director of Adult Education/Skills
Training
Northwest Shoals Community College
Muscle Shoals, Alabama

Jean Pierre-Pipkin, Ed.D.
Director of Beaumont I.S.D. Adult Education
Cooperative Consortium
Beaumont, Texas

STECK-VAUGHN

Harcourt Supplemental Publishers

www.steck-vaughn.com

Acknowledgments

Supervising Editor: Julie Higgins

Editor: Sharon Sargent

Associate Director of Design: Joyce Spicer

Supervising Designer: Pamela Heaney

Production Manager: Mychael Ferris

Production Coordinator: Heather Jernt

Senior Media Researcher: Alyx Kellington

Composition and Design: The Format Group, LLC

Photo Credits: P. iv ©Bluestone Productions/SuperStock Royalty Free; p. 2 ©HIRB/Index Stock Imagery; p. 4 ©Bob Daemmrich/The Image Works; p. 6 ©Spencer Grant/PhotoEdit; p. 69 ©Corbis Royalty Free.

ISBN 0-7398-8030-6

TABE® is a trademark of McGraw-Hill, Inc. Such company has neither endorsed nor authorized this publication.

Printed in the United States of America.

2 3 4 5 6 7 8 9 0 TPO 09 08 07 06 05 04

Contents

To the Learner

Congratulations on your decision to study for the TABE! You are taking an important step in your educational career. This book will help you do your best on the TABE. You'll also find hints and strategies that will help you prepare for test day. Practice these skills—your success lies in your hands.

What Is the TABE?

TABE stands for the Tests of Adult Basic Education. These paper-and-pencil tests, published by McGraw-Hill, measure your progress on basic skills. There are five tests in all: Reading, Mathematics Computation, Applied Mathematics, Language, and Spelling.

TABE Levels M, D, and A

Test	Number of Items	Suggested Working Time (in minutes)
1 **Reading**	50	50
2 **Mathematics Computation**	25	15
3 **Applied Mathematics**	50	50
4 **Language**	55	39
5 **Spelling**	20	10

Test 1 Reading

This test measures basic reading skills. The main concepts covered by this test are word meaning, critical thinking, and understanding basic information.

Many things on this test will look familiar to you. They include documents and forms necessary to your everyday life, such as directions, bank statements, maps, and consumer labels. The test also includes items that measure your ability to find and use information from a dictionary, table of contents, or library computer display. The TABE also tests a learner's understanding of fiction and nonfiction passages.

Test 2 Mathematics Computation

Test 2 covers adding, subtracting, multiplying, and dividing. On the test you must use these skills with whole numbers, fractions, decimals, integers, and percents.

The skills covered in the Mathematics Computation test are the same skills you use daily to balance your checkbook, double a recipe, or fix your car.

Test 3 | Applied Mathematics

The Applied Mathematics test links mathematical ideas to real-world situations. Many things you do every day require basic math. Making budgets, cooking, and doing your taxes all take math. The test covers pre-algebra, algebra, and geometry, too. Adults need to use all these skills.

Some questions will relate to one theme. Auto repairs could be the subject, for example. The question could focus on the repair schedule. For example, you know when you last had your car repaired. You also know how often you have to get it repaired. You might have to predict the next maintenance date.

Many of the items will not require you to use a specific strategy or formula to get the correct answer. Instead this test challenges you to use your own problem-solving strategies to answer the question.

Test 4 | Language

The Language test asks you to analyze different types of writing. Examples are business letters, resumes, job reports, and essays. For each task, you have to show you understand good writing skills.

The questions fit adult interests and concerns. Some questions ask you to think about what is wrong in the written material. In other cases, you will correct sentences and paragraphs.

Test 5 | Spelling

In everyday life, you need to spell correctly, especially in the workplace. The spelling words on this test are words that many people misspell and words that are commonly used in adult writing.

Test-Taking Tips

1. Read the directions very carefully. Make sure you read through them word for word. If you are not sure what the question says, ask the person giving the test to explain it to you.

2. Read each question carefully. Make sure you know what it means and what you have to do.

3. Read all of the answers carefully, even if you think you know the answer.

4. Make sure that the reading supports your answer. Don't answer without checking the reading. Don't rely only on outside knowledge.

5. Answer all of the questions. If you can't find the right answer, rule out the answers that you know are wrong. Then try to figure out the right answer. If you still don't know, make your best guess.

6. If you can't figure out the answer, put a light mark by the question and come back to it later. Erase your marks before you finish.

7. Don't change an answer unless you are sure your first answer is wrong. Usually your first idea is the correct answer.

8. If you get nervous, stop for a while. Take a few breaths and relax. Then start working again.

How to Use *TABE Fundamentals*

Step-by-Step Instruction In Levels M and D, each lesson starts with step-by-step instruction on a skill. The instruction contains examples and then a test example with feedback. This instruction is followed by practice questions. Work all of the questions in the lesson's practice and then check your work in the Answers and Explanations in the back of the book.

The Level A books contain practice for each skill covered on the TABE. Work all of the practice questions and then check your work in the Answers and Explanations in the back of the book.

Reviews The lessons in Levels M and D are grouped by a TABE Objective. At the end of each TABE Objective, there is a Review. Use these Reviews to find out if you need to review any of the lessons before continuing.

Performance Assessment At the end of every book, there is a special section called the Performance Assessment. This section is similar to the TABE test. It has the same number and type of questions. This assessment will give you an idea of what the real test is like.

Answer Sheet At the back of the book is a practice bubble-in answer sheet. Practice bubbling in your answers. Fill in the answer sheet carefully. For each answer, mark only one numbered space on the answer sheet. Mark the space beside the number that corresponds to the question. Mark only one answer per question. On the real TABE, if you have more than one answer per question, they will be scored as incorrect. Be sure to erase any stray marks.

Strategies and Hints Pay careful attention to the TABE Strategies and Hints throughout this book. Strategies are test-taking tips that help you do better on the test. Hints give you extra information about a skill.

Setting Goals

On the following page is a form to help you set your goals. Setting goals will help you get more from your work in this book.

Section 1. Why do you want to do well on the TABE? Take some time now to set your short-term and long-term goals on page 3.

Section 2. Making a schedule is one way to set priorities. Deadlines will help you stay focused on the steps you need to take to reach your goals.

Section 3. Your goals may change over time. This is natural. After a month, for example, check the progress you've made. Do you need to add new goals or make any changes to the ones you have? Checking your progress on a regular basis helps you reach your goals.

For more information on setting goals, see Steck-Vaughn's *Start Smart Goal Setting Strategies*.

1. Set Your Goals

What is your long-term goal for using this book?

_____
_____
_____

Complete these areas to identify the smaller steps to take to reach your long-term goal.

Content area	What I Know	What I Want to Learn
Reading	_____	_____
Language	_____	_____
Spelling	_____	_____
Math	_____	_____
Other	_____	_____

2. Make a Schedule

Set some deadlines for yourself.

For a 20-week planning calendar, see Steck-Vaughn's *Start Smart Planner.*

Goals	Begin Date	End Date
_____	_____	_____
_____	_____	_____
_____	_____	_____
_____	_____	_____

3. Celebrate Your Success

Note the progress you've made. If you made changes in your goals, record them here.

_____
_____
_____
_____

To the Instructor

About TABE 7 and 8

The Tests of Adult Basic Education are designed to meet the needs of adult learners in ABE programs. Written and designed to be relevant to adult learners' lives and interests, this material focuses on the life, job, academic, and problem-solving skills that the typical adult needs.

Because of the increasing importance of thinking skills in any curriculum, *TABE Fundamentals* focuses on critical thinking throughout each TABE Objective.

The TABE identifies the following thinking processes as essential to learning and achieving goals in daily life:

- ✦ Gather Information
- ✦ Organize Information
- ✦ Analyze Information
- ✦ Generate Ideas
- ✦ Synthesize Elements
- ✦ Evaluate Outcomes

Test 1 Reading

The TABE measures an adult's ability to understand home, workplace, and academic texts. The ability to construct meaning from prose and visual information is also covered through reading and analyzing diagrams, maps, charts, forms, and consumer materials.

Test 2 Mathematics Computation

This test covers whole numbers, decimals, fractions, integers, percents, and algebraic expressions. Skills are carefully targeted to the appropriate level of difficulty.

Test 3 Applied Mathematics

This test emphasizes problem-solving and critical-thinking skills, with a focus on the life-skill applications of mathematics. Estimation and pattern-recognition skills also are important on this test.

Test 4 Language

The Language test focuses on writing and effective communication. Students examine writing samples that need revision, with complete-sentence and paragraph contexts for the various items. The tests emphasize editing, proofreading, and other key skills. The context of the questions are real-life settings appropriate to adults.

Test 5 Spelling

This test focuses on the words learners most typically misspell. In this way, the test identifies the spelling skills learners most need in order to communicate effectively. Items typically present high-frequency words in short sentences.

Uses of the TABE

There are three basic uses of the TABE:

Instructional

From an instructional point of view, the TABE allows instructors to assess students' entry levels as they begin an adult program. The TABE also allows instructors to diagnose learners' strengths and weaknesses in order to determine appropriate areas to focus instruction. Finally the TABE allows instructors and institutions to monitor learners' progress.

Administrative

The TABE allows institutions to assess classes in general and measure the effectiveness of instruction and whether learners are making progress.

Governmental

The TABE provides a means of assessing a school's or program's effectiveness.

The National Reporting System (NRS) and the TABE

Adult education and literacy programs are federally funded and thus accountable to the federal government. The National Reporting System monitors adult education. Developed with the help of adult educators, the NRS sets the reporting requirements for adult education programs around the country. The information collected by the NRS is used to assess the effectiveness of adult education programs and make necessary improvements.

A key measure defined by the NRS is educational gain, which is an assessment of the improvement in learners' reading, writing, speaking, listening, and other skills during their instruction. Programs assess educational gain at every stage of instruction.

NRS Functioning Levels	Grade Levels	TABE (7–8) scaled scores
Beginning ABE Literacy	0–1.9	Reading . . . . 367 and below Total Math . . . . 313 and below Language . . . . . 391 and below
Beginning Basic Education	2–3.9	Reading . . . . 368–460 Total Math . . . . 393–490 Language 393–490
Low Intermediate Basic Education	4–5.9	Reading . . . . 461–517 Total Math . . . . 442–505 Language 491–523
High Intermediate Basic Education	6–8.9	Reading . . . . 518–566 Total Math . . . . 506–565 Language 524–559
Low Adult Secondary Education	9–10.9	Reading . . . . 567–595 Total Math . . . . 566–594 Language 560–585

According to the NRS guidelines, states select the method of assessment appropriate for their needs. States can assess educational gain either through standardized tests or through performance-based assessment. Among the standardized tests typically used under NRS guidelines is the TABE, which meets the NRS standards both for administrative procedures and for scoring.

The three main methods used by the NRS to collect data are the following:

1. **Direct program reporting,** from the moment of student enrollment
2. **Local follow-up surveys,** involving learners' employment or academic goals
3. **Data matching,** or sharing data among agencies serving the same clients so that outcomes unique to each program can be identified.

Two of the major goals of the NRS are academic achievement and workplace readiness. Educational gain is a means to reaching these goals. As learners progress through the adult education curriculum, the progress they make should help them either obtain or keep employment or obtain a diploma, whether at the secondary school level or higher. The TABE is flexible enough to meet both the academic and workplace goals set forth by the NRS.

Using *TABE Fundamentals*

Adult Basic Education Placement

From the outset, the TABE allows effective placement of learners. You can use the *TABE Fundamentals* series to support instruction of those skills where help is needed.

High School Equivalency

Placement often involves predicting learners' success on the GED, the high school equivalency exam. Each level of *TABE Fundamentals* covers Reading, Language, Spelling, Applied and Computational Math to allow learners to focus their attention where it is needed.

Assessing Progress

Each TABE skill is covered in a lesson. These lessons are grouped by TABE Objective. At the end of each TABE Objective, there is a Review. Use these Reviews to find out if the learners need to review any of the skills before continuing.

At the end of the book, there is a special section called the Performance Assessment. This section is similar to the TABE test. It has the same number and type of questions. You can use the Performance Assessment as a timed pretest or posttest with your learners, or as a more general review for the actual TABE.

Steck-Vaughn's *TABE Fundamentals* Program at a Glance

The charts on the following page provide a quick overview of the elements of Steck-Vaughn's *TABE Fundamentals* series. Use this chart to match the TABE objectives with the skill areas for each level. This chart will come in handy whenever you need to find which objectives fit the specific skill areas you need to cover.

Steck-Vaughn's *TABE Fundamentals* Program at a Glance

TABE OBJECTIVE	Level M		Level D		Level A
	Reading	Language and Spelling	Reading	Language and Spelling	Reading, Language, and Spelling
Reading					
Interpret Graphic Information	✦		✦		✦
Words in Context	✦		✦		✦
Recall Information	✦		✦		✦
Construct Meaning	✦		✦		✦
Evaluate/Extend Meaning	✦		✦		✦
Language					
Usage		✦		✦	✦
Sentence Formation		✦		✦	✦
Paragraph Development		✦		✦	✦
Punctuation and Capitalization		✦		✦	✦
Writing Convention		✦		✦	✦
Spelling					
Vowel		✦		✦	✦
Consonant		✦		✦	✦
Structural Unit		✦		✦	✦

	Level M		Level D		Level A
	Math Computation	Applied Math	Math Computation	Applied Math	Computational and Applied Math
Mathematics Computation					
Addition of Whole Numbers	✦				
Subtraction of Whole Numbers	✦				
Multiplication of Whole Numbers	✦		✦		
Division of Whole Numbers	✦		✦		
Decimals	✦		✦		✦
Fractions	✦		✦		✦
Integers			✦		✦
Percents			✦		✦
Algebraic Operations					✦
Applied Mathematics					
Numeration		✦		✦	
Number Theory		✦		✦	
Data Interpretation		✦		✦	
Pre-Algebra and Algebra		✦		✦	
Measurement		✦		✦	
Geometry		✦		✦	
Computation in Context		✦		✦	
Estimation		✦		✦	

Lesson 1 | Word Names

Odometers and scales are two places you may regularly see large numbers with decimals displayed. It's important to learn to read the written form of large numbers that include decimals. You can make a place-value chart to help you find the written form of large numbers on the TABE.

Example **The tallest mountain in Colorado is Mt. Elbert with an elevation of about 14,432.4 feet. How is Mt. Elbert's elevation written in word form?**

Step 1. Set up place-value chart to help you find the value of each digit.

ten thousands	thousands	hundreds	tens	ones	decimal point	tenths
10,000s	1,000s	100s	10s	1s		10ths
The value of the 1 is 10,000.	The value of the 4 is 4000.	The value of the 4 is 400.	The value of the 3 is 30.	The value of the 2 is 2.	and	The value of the 4 is four tenths.
1	4	4	3	2	.	4

Step 2. Begin reading the number from left to right. Read the number to the left of the decimal just as you would any number. The number to the left is 14, 432. Write that just as you would say it, fourteen thousand four hundred thirty-two.

Step 3. Read the decimal as "and."

Step 4. Now read the number to the right of the decimal. It reads just like any other number except that the name of the place is added, "tenths." The number is read as "4 tenths."

Mt. Elbert is fourteen thousand four hundred thirty-two and four tenths feet high.

Test Example

Read the question. Circle the answer.

1   The scale shows the combined weight of 7 cartons of freight at 41,025.8 pounds. How is this written in words?

| 4 | 1 | 0 | 2 | 5 | 8 |

A   four hundred ten thousand two hundred fifty-eight

B   forty-one thousand two hundred fifty-eight

C   forty-one thousand twenty-five and eight tenths

D   forty-one thousand two hundred fifty and eight tenths

TABE Strategy

Write your answer in a place-value chart. Then check to see if it matches the word form of the number.

1 **C** The written form of 41,025.8 is forty-one thousand twenty-five and eight tenths.

ten thousands	thousands	hundreds	tens	ones	decimal point	tenths
10,000s	1,000s	100s	10s	1s		10ths
4	1	0	2	5	.	8

Practice

Read the question. Circle the answer.

1 The picture shows the odometer of a school bus. What is the mileage shown on the odometer?

| 6 | 3 | 0 | 7 | 2 | 4 |

A six hundred thousand seventy-two and four tenths

B sixty-three thousand seventy-two and four tenths

C six thousand three hundred seventy-two and four tenths

D sixty-three hundred seventy-two and four tenths

2 Last year, the farmers in one county harvested 75,058.6 bushels of corn. Which of the following represents the number of bushels the farmers harvested?

F seventy hundred fifty thousand fifty-eight and six tenths

G seventy-five thousand five hundred eighty and six tenths

H seventy-five thousand eighty-five and six tenths

J seventy-five thousand fifty-eight and six tenths

3 Which of the following numbers is the same as 89,048.3?

A eight hundred-ninety thousand forty-eight and three tenths

B eighty-nine thousand four hundred eighty and three tenths

C eighty-nine thousand forty-eight and three tenths

D eighty-nine thousand four hundred eighty-three

4 Which of the following numbers is the same as 64,103.7?

F sixty-four thousand one hundred three and seven tenths

G six hundred four thousand one hundred three and seven tenths

H sixty-four thousand one hundred thirty and seven tenths

J sixty-four thousand one hundred thirty and seven tenths

TABE Strategy

Read each option to yourself before circling the answer.

Check your answers on page 116.

Lesson 2 Recognizing Numbers

Numbers can be expressed in various ways, with numerals, with words, and with a combination of words and numerals. Numbers can also be expressed using parenthesis to group them. On the TABE you will see numbers written in different forms.

Example **What are some ways to show 406?**

Step 1. Think of some ways to show or name numbers.

in standard form	406
as addition	400 + 6
in words	four hundred six
in numerals and words	4 hundred 6

Step 2. Numbers can also be shown by their place values. Set up a place-value chart and find the value of each digit. Add the place value of each digit to show another form.

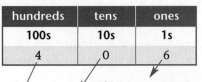

hundreds	tens	ones
100s	10s	1s
4	0	6

The 6 means 6 ones, or **6 × 1**
The 0 means no tens, or **0 × 10**
The 4 means 4 hundred, or **4 × 100**

$$(4 \times 100) + (0 \times 10) + (6 \times 1) = 406$$

Step 3. To make this form easier to read, you can group the numbers being multiplied in parentheses. Because 0 × 10 = 0, you don't have to include it.

$$(4 \times 100) + (6 \times 1)$$

To check to be sure you've grouped the numbers correctly, solve the operation in the parentheses first, then add.

$$(4 \times 100) = \mathbf{400}$$
$$(6 \times 1) = \underline{+\ 6}$$
$$\mathbf{406}$$

Another form of 406 is (4 × 100) + (6 × 1).

Test Example

Read the question. Circle the answer.

1   Sound travels at one thousand five hundred thirty-one meters per second while passing through salt water. Which of the following choices shows the same number?

A   153

B   1531

C   1351

D   1135

Practice

Read the question. Circle the answer.

1 Which of these numbers is four hundred eight thousand two hundred fifty-six?

A 480,256

B 48,256

C 408,256

D 482,560

2 Which of these is another way to show 307?

F three hundred seven

G 30 + 7

H $(3 \times 100) + (7 \times 10)$

J 3 hundreds 7 tens

3 The driving distance from New York to Los Angeles is two thousand seven hundred ninety-seven miles. Which number shows this distance?

A 2979

B 2727

C 2779

D 2797

4 Which is another way to show 840?

F eight hundred four

G $(8 \times 100) + (4 \times 10)$

H 4 hundred 80 four

J 800 + 4

5 A cable company has 50,093 customers. What is another way to show this number?

A fifty thousand ninety-three

B fifty thousand nine hundred three

C fifty-nine thousand three

D thirty-nine thousand fifty

6 Which of these is another way to show 407?

F four hundred seven

G $(4 \times 100) + (7 \times 10)$

H 40 + 7

J four hundreds seven tens

TABE Strategy

Four-digit numbers are written without a comma on the TABE.

Check your answers on page 116.

Lesson 3 · Expanded Notation

Expanded notation is another way to show numbers. Expanded notation shows the actual value of each digit in a number. On the TABE you will have to identify numbers written in expanded notation.

Example **Last year, about 9,899,800 sport utility vehicles were sold. How would this number be written in expanded notation?**

Step 1. Each digit must be assigned a place value. Write the number in a place-value chart.

millions	hundred thousands	ten thousands	thousands	hundreds	tens	ones
1,000,000s	100,000s	10,000s	1,000s	100s	10s	0
9	8	9	9	8	0	0

Step 2. Multiply each number by its place value:

$9 \times 1,000,000 = 9,000,000$
$8 \times 100,000 = 800,000$
$9 \times 10,000 = 90,000$
$9 \times 1,000 = 9,000$
$8 \times 100 = 800$

Step 3. Check your work by adding the numbers.

$$
\begin{array}{r}
9,000,000 \\
800,000 \\
90,000 \\
9,000 \\
+800 \\
\hline
9,899,800
\end{array}
$$

9,899,800 in expanded notation is 9,000,000 + 800,000 + 90,000 + 9,000 + 800.

Test Example

Read the question. Circle the answer.

1   A number is written as 3,000,000 + 40,000 + 300 + 60 + 5.
What is another way to show this number?

A   3,430,365

B   3,400,635

C   3,044,635

D   3,040,365

Hint

When adding, make sure the digits are lined up by place value.

1 **D** 3,000,000 + 40,000 + 300 + 60 + 5 is written as
3,040,000,365.

```
      3,000,000
         40,000
            300
             60
    +         5
    _____
      3,040,365
```

Practice

Read the question. Circle the answer.

1 Which of these is another way to write
40,000,000 + 1,000,000 + 9?

A 40,100,009

B 41,000,090

C 40,001,900

D 41,000,009

2 What is another way to show 35,069?

F 30,000 + 5,000 + 60 + 9

G 30,000 + 6,000 + 50 + 9

H 50,000 + 3,000 + 60 + 9

J 30,000 + 5,000 + 90 + 6

3 The distance of Earth from the Sun
may be expressed as 90,000,000 +
2,000,000 + 900,000 + 50,000 +
5,000 + 800 miles. How many miles is
earth from the sun?

A 92,855,900

B 92,955,080

C 92,955,800

D 95,529,800

4 The season's attendance for a hockey
team was 800,000 + 6,000 + 500 +
90 + 3. What is another way to show
this number?

F 860,593

G 806,593

H 806,953

J 809,563

5 According to the 2000 census, the
population of Illinois was 12,419,293.
How could the population of Illinois be
written in extended notation?

A 10,000,000 + 4,000,000 + 200,000 +
10,000 + 9,000 + 200 + 90 + 3

B 10,000,000 + 2,000,000 + 400,000 +
10,000 + 9,000 + 200 + 90 + 3

C 10,000,000 + 2,000,000 + 100,000 +
40,000 + 9,000 + 200 + 90 + 3

D 10,000,000 + 2,000,000 + 400,000 +
10,000 + 9,000 + 900 + 20 + 3

6 Which number does 500,000 + 6,000 +
400 + 80 represent?

F 560,480

G 560,408

H 506,480

J 506,048

Check your answers on page 116.

Comparison

You compare amounts every day. For example, when you want to choose the best hitter on a baseball team, you probably compare batting averages. This lesson will help you compare decimals and fractions on the TABE.

Example The batting averages for four players are 0.358, 0.338, 0.372, and 0.368. Which batting average is the highest?

Step 1. Write all the numbers in a column, lining up the numbers by the decimal points. Compare the numbers in each column. The ones column has all 0s, and the tenths column has all 3s.

> 0.358
> 0.338
> 0.372
> 0.368

Step 2. Compare the numbers in the next column to the right. Because 7 is the greatest number in the column, you don't need to compare the numbers in the next column. 0.372 is the highest batting average.

> 0.358
> 0.338
> 0.372
> 0.368

The highest batting average is 0.372.

Example Mike lost $\frac{1}{2}$ inch, Tara lost $\frac{1}{3}$ inch, Simone lost $\frac{1}{4}$ inch, and Jake lost $\frac{3}{4}$ inch. Who lost the most on their weight-loss program?

Step 1. Draw the fractions.

This shows $\frac{1}{2}$ inch, or how much Mike lost.

This shows $\frac{1}{3}$ inch, or how much Tara lost.

This shows $\frac{1}{4}$ inch, or how much Simone lost.

This shows $\frac{3}{4}$ inch, or how much Jake lost.

Step 2. Compare the shaded areas. Which bar has the most shading? The bar labeled $\frac{3}{4}$ inch has the most shading.

Jake lost the most because the $\frac{3}{4}$-inch bar has the greatest amount of shading.

Example Compare $\frac{1}{3}$ and $\frac{3}{2}$ to determine which fraction is less than or greater than 1.

Step 1. Look at the top number of the fraction $\frac{1}{3}$. If the top number is smaller than the bottom number, the fraction is less than 1.

Step 2. Look at the top number of the fraction $\frac{3}{2}$. If the top number is greater than the bottom number, the fraction is greater than 1.

$\frac{1}{3}$ is less than 1. $\frac{3}{2}$ is greater than 1. Therefore, $\frac{3}{2}$ is greater than $\frac{1}{3}$.

Test Example

Read the question. Circle the answer.

1 To make Chicken with Lemon Sauce, the cafeteria cook needs $\frac{6}{4}$ cups chicken stock, $\frac{1}{4}$ cup parsley, $\frac{1}{2}$ cup lemon juice, and $\frac{3}{4}$ cup of chopped onions. Which ingredient amount is greater than 1 cup?

A lemon juice   C chicken stock

B parsley   D onions

TABE Strategy

When reading fractions, read the top and bottom numbers carefully before you choose an answer.

1 **C** Chicken stock, $\frac{6}{4}$ cups. Its amount is the only one in which the top number of the fraction is larger than its bottom number.

Practice

Read the question. Circle the answer.

1 Which of these decimals is less than 0.638 and greater than 0.621?

A 0.649

B 0.613

C 0.635

D 0.620

2 How many of the fractions in the box are less than 1?

$$\frac{7}{8}, \frac{9}{7}, \frac{3}{5}, \frac{7}{6}, \frac{3}{4}$$

F 3

G 2

H 4

J 1

3 The precipitation amount for New York City on April 1, 2002 was 0.69 inches. On the same day in 2003, 0.76 inches were recorded. Which amount would be greater than the 2002 total, but less than the 2003 amount?

A 0.84

B 0.77

C 0.68

D 0.74

Check your answers on page 116.

Fractional Part

A store is having a "50% off" sale. Another store is having a similar sale but their sign says " $\frac{1}{2}$ off sale." The fraction $\frac{1}{2}$ is the same as 50%, so you know that you'll save the same at each store.

Example   **Jeff has painted 6 of the 10 rooms in his house. In simplest terms, what fraction of the rooms in his house has Jeff painted?**

Step 1. Set up a fraction, $\frac{6}{10}$. Find a number that will go into, or divide, both 6 and 10 evenly. Since there are three 2s in 6 (or $3 \times 2 = 6$) and five 2s in 10 (or $5 \times 2 = 10$), we can say that 2 will go into, or divide, both 6 and 10 evenly.

Step 2. Reduce the fraction by dividing the top number and the bottom number by 2.

$$\frac{6}{10} \div \frac{2}{2} = \frac{3}{5}$$

Step 3. Can the fraction be reduced anymore? No, because there is no number that can divide both 3 and 5 evenly. The fraction is in its simplest form.

Jeff has painted $\frac{3}{5}$ of the rooms in his house.

Example   **About 20% of the air you breathe is oxygen. What fraction of the air is oxygen?**

Step 1. Write 20% as a fraction. Because "%" means "out of 100 parts" you can convert the 20% to a fraction by deleting the percent sign and putting 20 over 100.

$$20\% = \frac{20}{100}$$

Step 2. Reduce 20/100. Find a number that will divide both 20 and 100 evenly. Because there is one **20** in 20 and there are five **20**s in 100, divide 20 and 100 by 20.

$$\frac{20}{100} \div \frac{20}{20} = \frac{1}{5}$$

$\frac{1}{5}$ of the air you breathe is oxygen.

Test Example

1   A state park saw 30% more families visit this year than last year. What fraction shows how many more families visited the park this year?

A $\frac{3}{10}$ C $\frac{3}{33}$

B $\frac{1}{3}$ D $\frac{5}{20}$

Can the top and bottom number be divided by the same number? If so, then the fraction can be reduced.

1 A Write 30% as a fraction. Find a number that will divide 30 and 100 evenly. Then divide.

$$\frac{30}{100} \div \frac{10}{10} = \frac{3}{10}$$

Practice

This diagram shows the plans for a new football stadium. Study the diagram. Then do number 1.

1 What fractional part of the east section of the football stadium will have luxury seating?

A $\frac{1}{3}$

B $\frac{1}{6}$

C $\frac{1}{4}$

D $\frac{1}{2}$

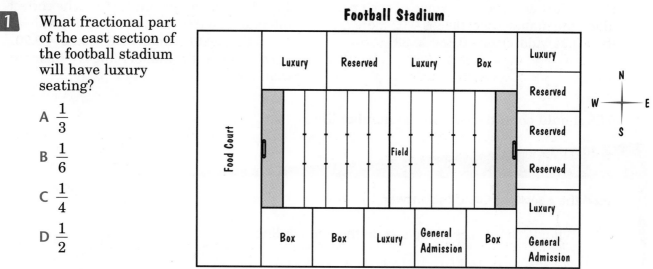

This map shows the roads in Albertson. Study the map. Then do number 2.

2 The length of Netz Place is what fraction of the length of Willis Avenue?

F $\frac{1}{2}$

G $\frac{1}{3}$

H $\frac{1}{4}$

J $\frac{1}{5}$

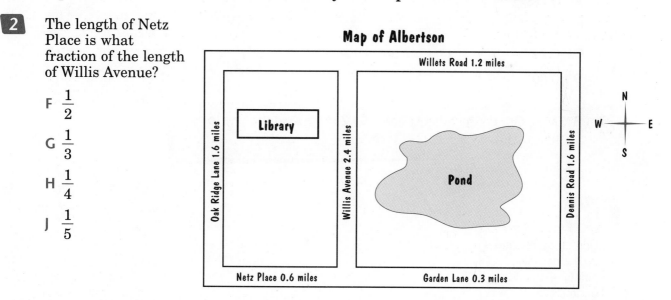

Check your answers on page 116.

Lesson 6 | Number Line

You can use a number line to show the relationships between whole numbers, fractions, or decimals. A number line is a line that has points at regular intervals, and each point has an assigned value. On the TABE you will solve problems using a number line.

Example What decimal goes in the box on the number line?

0.84 0.86 ☐ 0.90 0.92 0.94 0.96 0.98

Step 1. First decide on the value of each point along the number line. 0.86 is 0.02 more than 0.84. Add. 0.02 + 0.86 = 0.88

Step 2. To make sure that 0.02 is the correct interval, add 0.02 to 0.88 to see if it will equal the next decimal. 0.88 + 0.02 = 0.90. Each point on the number line is 0.02 more than the one to the left of it.

0.88 should go in the box on the number line.

Test Example

Read the question. Circle the answer.

1 What decimal goes in the box on the number line?

0.71 0.73 ☐ 0.81

A 0.77

B 0.75

C 0.74

D 0.80

1 B Each point on the number line is 0.02 more than the one to the left of it. 0.73 + 0.02 = 0.75.

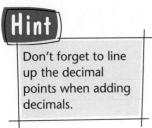

Hint

Don't forget to line up the decimal points when adding decimals.

Applied Math

Read the question. Circle the answer.

1 What decimal goes in the box on the number line?

0.53 0.54   □   0.61

    A 0.59   C 0.57

    B 0.58   D 0.60

2 What decimal goes in the box on the number line?

0.01 0.02   □   0.09

    F 0.50   H 0.04

    G 0.60   J 0.05

3 What decimal goes in the box on the number line?

0.05   □   0.15

    A 0.09   C 0.11

    B 0.07   D 0.90

4 What decimal goes in the box on the number line?

0.66 0.70 0.74   □   0.98

    F 0.86   H 0.80

    G 0.84   J 0.76

5 What decimal goes in the box on the number line?

0.37   0.43   □   0.49

    A 0.47   C 0.48

    B 0.46   D 0.45

6 What decimal goes in the box on the number line?

0.55   0.57   □

    F 0.58   H 0.60

    G 0.59   J 0.61

7 Steve recorded daily snowfall totals for the past five days on this chart.

Weekly Snowfall

Day	Total Snowfall for week
Monday	0.02 inches
Tuesday	0.03 inches
Wednesday	0.06 inches
Thursday	0.08 inches
Friday	0.10 inches

He wanted to use a number line to plot the amount and the day. Which day would be at 0.06?

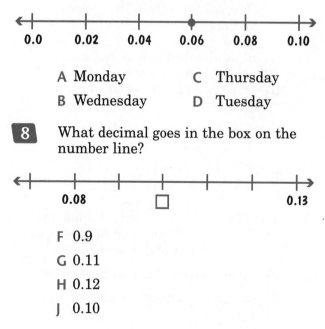

0.0   0.02   0.04   0.06   0.08   0.10

    A Monday   C Thursday

    B Wednesday   D Tuesday

8 What decimal goes in the box on the number line?

0.08   □   0.13

    F 0.9

    G 0.11

    H 0.12

    J 0.10

Check your answers on page 116.

Solve. Circle the answer.

1 Which of these numbers is three hundred sixty thousand three hundred ninety-five?

A 36,395

B 306,935

C 360,395

D 306,395

2 The picture shows the number of miles on Craig's car odometer. What is the mileage shown on the odometer?

F thirty-five thousand twenty-eight and seven tenths

G thirty-five thousand seven hundred twenty and eight tenths

H thirty-five thousand two hundred seven and eight tenths

J thirty-five thousand twenty-seven and eight tenths

3 Of all adults dining in a restaurant, 40% chose the daily special. What fraction of adults chose the daily special?

A $\frac{1}{5}$ **C** $\frac{1}{4}$

B $\frac{2}{5}$ **D** $\frac{3}{4}$

4 The CN Tower in Toronto, Canada, is 1815 feet tall. What is another way to show the height of the tower?

F eight thousand one hundred five feet

G one thousand eight hundred fifty feet

H one thousand eight hundred fifteen feet

J one thousand four hundred eight feet

The diagram shows Mel's plan for his new garden. The sections with vegetables are labeled V. The sections with flowers are labeled F. Study the diagram. Then do number 5.

F	V	V	V	F	F
F	V	V	V	F	F
F	V	V	F	F	F
F	V	V	F	F	F

5 What fractional part of the garden will be planted in flowers?

A $\frac{7}{10}$ **C** $\frac{12}{24}$

B $\frac{4}{14}$ **D** $\frac{7}{12}$

6 Which of these is another way to show 50,000 + 6,000 + 800 + 80 + 9?

F 56,889

G 55,999

H 56,898

J 56,890

7 Which of these numbers is three thousand five hundred eight?

A 3508

B 3580

C 358

D 3058

8 How many of the fractions in the box are greater than 1?

$$\frac{3}{8}, \frac{9}{10}, \frac{5}{4}, \frac{3}{2}, \frac{14}{15}$$

F 5   **H** 1

G 3   **J** 2

9 Inside a personal computer, 5 memory chips fit inside a 1-inch section. How much space do 3 memory chips take up?

A $\frac{4}{5}$ inch

B $\frac{5}{3}$ inch

C $\frac{3}{5}$ inch

D $\frac{5}{5}$ inch

10 What decimal goes in the box on the number line?

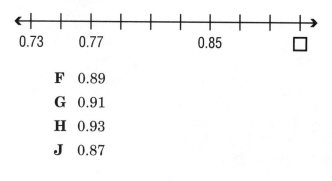

F 0.89

G 0.91

H 0.93

J 0.87

11 In a single day, 10,000,000 + 3,000,000 + 700,000 + 60,000 + 4,000 shares of a company's stock were traded. Which is another way to write this number?

A 31,764,000

B 13,764,000

C 13,746,000

D 13,674,000

12 What decimal goes in the box on the number line?

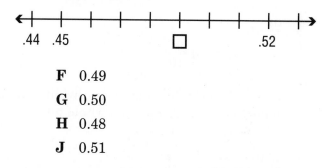

F 0.49

G 0.50

H 0.48

J 0.51

13 The distance around Pine Lake is 4 miles. The distance around Keystone Lake is 12 miles. The distance around Pine Lake is what fraction of the distance around Keystone Lake?

A $\frac{1}{8}$

B $\frac{1}{3}$

C $\frac{1}{2}$

D $\frac{2}{3}$

14 Which of these decimals is less than 0.561 and greater than 0.503?

F 0.591

G 0.053

H 0.503

J 0.519

Check your answers on pages 116–117

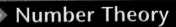
Lesson 7 Equivalent Form

The word "equivalent" means "the same." The jogging path around a lake is $1\frac{1}{4}$ miles. If you jog around the lake, you can say that you jogged $1\frac{1}{4}$ miles or 1.25 miles. The fraction $1\frac{1}{4}$ is equivalent to, or the same as, 1.25. On the TABE you will convert decimals into fractions.

Example The drive from Miguel's home to his workplace is 4.8 miles. What is another way to write the distance Miguel travels?

Step 1. Write the decimal as a whole number and a fraction. The decimal 0.8 can be written as $\frac{8}{10}$.

$$4.8 = 4\frac{8}{10}$$

Step 2. Reduce the fraction by dividing the top number and the bottom number by 2. You don't have to do anything to the whole number.

$$4\frac{8}{10} \div \frac{2}{2} = \frac{4}{5} \longrightarrow 4\frac{4}{5}$$

Another way to write 4.8 miles is $4\frac{4}{5}$ miles.

Test Example

Read the question. Circle the answer.

1 What is another way to write 2.6?

A twenty six

B $2\frac{3}{5}$

C $2\frac{2}{5}$

D three and six tenths

1 **B** 2.6 can be written as $2\frac{6}{10}$ or $2\frac{3}{5}$. $2.6 = 2\frac{6}{10}$. $\frac{6}{10} \div \frac{2}{2} = \frac{3}{5}$. $2\frac{6}{10} = 2\frac{3}{5}$. Option A is 26. Option C is 2.4. Option D is $3\frac{6}{10}$ or 3.6.

This chart shows the heights of five friends. Study the chart. Then do number 1.

5.25 ft. 6.00 ft. 5.67 ft.   5.5 ft.   5.33 ft.

Sonia   Donnell   Phillip   Ellen   Mike

1 Which of these is another way to write Ellen's height?

A five-twelfths feet

B $\frac{51}{100}$ feet

C five and three tenths feet

D $5\frac{1}{2}$ feet

Read the question. Circle the answer.

2 If 0.35 of all pets are dogs, what fraction of pets are dogs?

F three tenths   H $1\frac{3}{20}$

G $\frac{7}{20}$ J one-third

3 With the rapid growth of industries in the United States, there was a great increase in steel production from 1880 to 1900.

Steel Production

Year	Increase
1880 – 1885	0.75
1885 – 1890	0.70
1890 – 1895	0.78
1895 – 1900	0.79

Which time period had the smallest increase in steel production?

A 1885 – 1890   C 1880 – 1885

B 1890 – 1895   D 1895 – 2000

4 Of all customers at a restaurant, 0.25 are children. What fractional part of customers are children?

F two and one half

G $\frac{1}{4}$

H one and one fourth

J $\frac{2}{100}$

5 In the town of Mayfield, thirty adults signed up to tutor high school students. The chart below shows their subjects.

High-School Tutors

Subject	Portion of Tutors
Math	$\frac{1}{6}$
Reading	$\frac{2}{10}$
Social Studies	$\frac{1}{10}$
Science	$\frac{1}{15}$
Spanish	$\frac{4}{15}$
Study Skills	$\frac{1}{5}$

Which 2 subjects will have the same number of tutors?

A Study Skills and Social Studies

B Spanish and Reading

C Reading and Study Skills

D Science and Social Studies

6 A survey at a shoe store found that 0.75 of shoppers preferred to shop on Saturday. What fraction shows the number of the customers who preferred to shop on Saturday?

F $\frac{3}{4}$ H one and seven fifths

G fifty-seven hundreds   J $1\frac{1}{4}$

Check your answers on page 117.

Lesson 8 ▸ Ratio and Proportion

You come in contact with ratios every day. Whenever you see the words "nine out of ten" or "miles to the gallon," or "1 inch = 5 miles," you are reading a ratio.

A ratio is a comparison of two numbers, and it can be written as a fraction. For example, if the scale on a map represents 1 inch for every 5 miles, you can say that the ratio of inches to miles is 1 inch = 5 miles, or $\frac{1}{5}$.

Example Angie has a planter that measures 4 feet long, 2 feet wide and 3 feet high. She makes another planter that is proportional to it but has a length of 12 inches. What is the width and height of the new planter?

Step 1. Determine the scale Angie used to create the second planter. Because the new planter will be in inches, convert all measurements of the old planter to inches. There are 12 inches in a foot, so multiply the number of feet by 12 to get the number of inches.

Step 2. Set up a ratio of the old length and the new one as a fraction: $\frac{48}{12}$

length is **4** feet × **12** = 48 inches
width is **2** feet × **12** = 24 inches
height is **3** feet × **12** = 36 inches

Step 3. Reduce the fraction to its lowest terms. Divide the top and bottom numbers by 12.

$$\frac{48}{12} \div \frac{12}{12} = \frac{4}{1}$$

The ratio of the old planter length to the new planter length is 4 inches (old planter) = 1 inch (new planter), $\frac{4}{1}$.

Step 4. Set up a proportion to find the width of the new planter. Let w stand for the width of the new planter. We know that the old planter is 24 inches wide.

$$\frac{4 \text{ inches (length of \textbf{old planter})}}{1 \text{ inch (length of \textbf{new planter})}} = \frac{24 \text{ inches (width of \textbf{old planter})}}{w \text{ inches (width of \textbf{new planter})}}$$

Now find out what number multiplied by 4 equals 24. 24 ÷ 4 = 6. That number is 6. Multiply the top and the bottom by 6. 4 × 6 = 24. Multiply 1 inch × 6 to get the width of the new planter.

$$\frac{4}{1} \times \frac{6}{6} = \frac{24 \text{ inches}}{6 \text{ inches}} \text{ (\textbf{width of new planter})}$$

Step 5. Set up a proportion to find the height of the new planter. Let h stand for the height of the new planter. We know that the old planter is 36 inches high.

$$\frac{4 \text{ inches (length of \textbf{old planter})}}{1 \text{ inch (length of \textbf{new planter})}} = \frac{36 \text{ inches (height of \textbf{old planter})}}{h \text{ inches (height of \textbf{new planter})}}$$

Now find out what number multiplied by 4 equals 36. 36 ÷ 4 = 9. That number is 9. 9 × 4 = 36. Multiply the top and bottom numbers by 9 to get the height of the new planter.

$$\frac{4}{1} \times \frac{9}{9} = \frac{36 \text{ inches}}{9 \text{ inches}} \text{ (\textbf{height of new planter})}$$

The width of the new planter is 6 inches and the height is 9 inches.

Read the question. Circle the answer.

1 Carmen is building a shed. The blueprints show that a 3-inch line represents a 12-foot side. What scale was used to draw the blueprint?

- **A** 3 inches = 10 feet
- **B** 3 inches = $\frac{1}{2}$ foot
- **C** 1 inch = 4 feet
- **D** 1 inch = 3 feet

Hint

For a proportion, the terms in both ratios have to be kept in the same order. Be sure that you are comparing inches to inches and feet to feet.

1 C The ratio 3 inches = 12 feet can be written as $\frac{3}{12}$. It can be reduced by dividing each number by 3.

$$\frac{3 \text{ inches}}{12 \text{ feet}} \div \frac{3}{3} = \frac{1 \text{ inch}}{4 \text{ feet}}$$

Practice

Sarah wants to build a new back patio. This diagram shows the dimensions of the patio. Study the diagram. Then answer numbers 1 and 2.

1 A 2-inch line in the diagram represents 6 feet of the patio. What scale is used to draw the diagram?

A 1 inch = 6 feet

B 1 inch = 3 feet

C 1 inch = 2 feet

D I inch = 8 feet

2 Sarah's neighbor Stan wants a new patio for his yard like Sarah's. His patio will have a length of 22 feet. What will be the width of the larger patio?

F   6 feet

G   4 feet

H 15 feet

J   20 feet

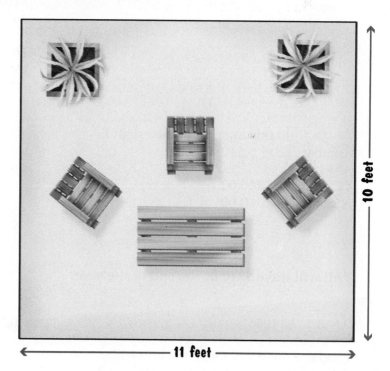

10 feet

11 feet

Check your answers on page 117.

You come in contact with percents every day. Sales tax, inflation rates, and discounts are a few examples. Percents can be written as a fraction. They are always over 100 because percent means "out of a hundred" parts. Knowing how to use percents can be helpful in solving many types of problems both in everyday life and on the TABE.

Example **Phil put $200 in the bank where it will pay 5% interest per year. How much money will he have at the bank after one year?**

Step 1. Change the percent to a decimal. First drop the "%" sign. There's no decimal point, so put one at the right of the number 5. Then move the decimal point two places to the left

$$5\% \longrightarrow 5. \longrightarrow .05$$

Step 2. Multiply the numbers as if they were both whole numbers.

$$
\begin{array}{r}
200 \\
\times\ \ \ 5 \\
\hline
1000
\end{array}
$$

Step 3. Count the places to the right of the decimal point in each number.

$$200. \longrightarrow \textbf{0} \text{ decimal places}$$
$$0.05 \longrightarrow \underline{+\ 2} \text{ decimal places}$$
$$\qquad\qquad \textbf{2} \text{ decimal places}$$

Step 4. Add the number of decimal places to find the total number of decimal places. Starting at the right of the answer, count to the left the total number of decimal places. Then place the decimal point.

$$1000 \longrightarrow 10.00$$
$$\$10.00$$
2 decimal places

The amount of interest paid is $10.00.

Hint

Sometimes you'll need to fill places with zeros when placing the decimal in a multiplication problem.

Step 5. Add this amount to the original number: $200 + $10 = $210.

$$
\begin{array}{r}
\$200.00 \\
+\ \$\ 10.00 \\
\hline
\$210.00
\end{array}
$$

Step 6. You may also write 5% as a fraction and set up a proportion. Then add that number to the original number.

$$5\% = \frac{5}{100} = \frac{\$}{200} \longrightarrow \frac{5}{100} \times \frac{2}{2} = \frac{10}{200}$$

Phil will have $210 at the end of the year.

Test Example

Read the question. Circle the answer.

1 Full-grown Indian elephants can be 10 feet tall. African elephants are about 30% taller. About how tall is an African elephant?

A 16 feet

B 11 feet

C 15 feet

D 13 feet

1 D Change 30% to 0.30 and multiply this by the size of the Indian elephant: 10 feet × 0.30 = 3 feet. To find the size of the African elephant, add 10 feet + 3 feet = 13 feet.

Practice

Read the question. Circle the answer.

1 A CD player sells for $95.99. The sales tax is 7%. What is the total cost for 2 CD players?

A $205.42

B $204.36

C $215.63

D $102.71

2 Emanuel pays 5% of his monthly salary of $2495.55 to his health-care plan. To compute this payment, he must multiply $2495.55 by

F 0.005

G 0.5

H 0.05

J 0.0005

3 A snow-removal service offered a one-time special of 20% off their regular fee of $30 per hour. What was the snow removal fee for 103 hours of work?

A $2090.00

B $2472.00

C $2137.00

D $2060.00

Study this advertisement for a sale. Then do numbers 4 and 5.

4 There is a 6% sales tax. If you pay cash, what is the total cost of the blouse with tax?

F $53.00   H $54.00

G $52.00   J $56.00

5 If you buy the blouse through the installment plan, what is the amount of the down payment?

A $8.00   C $6.00

B $12.00   D $10.00

Check your answers on page 117.

Solve. Circle the answer.

1 What is another way to write 2.6?

  A $\dfrac{6}{10}$

  B $2\dfrac{3}{5}$

  C Two and six-hundredths

  D $2\dfrac{6}{100}$

2 Kevin adds a 10% tip to his bill at the restaurant. To compute this tip, he should multiply $14.50 by

  F 0.10   **H** 0.0001

  G 0.01   **J** 1.00

The United States measures about 3000 miles from east to west and 2000 miles from north to south. Karen wants to draw a map of the United States.

3 Two inches on the map represents 600 miles. What scale was used to draw the map?

  A 2 inches = 3000 miles

  B 2 inches = 300 miles

  C 1 inch = 300 miles

  D 1 inch = 600 miles

4 Karen plans to draw a map of one section of the country, using the same proportions as the larger map. If the actual distance from north to south of this section is 1000 miles, what is the actual distance of the section from east to west?

  F 2000 miles

  G 1500 miles

  H 2500 miles

  J 1000 miles

5 If 0.25 of people chose pizza as their favorite lunch, what fraction of people chose pizza?

  A $\dfrac{1}{3}$ **C** $\dfrac{1}{2}$

  B $\dfrac{2}{5}$ **D** $\dfrac{1}{4}$

6 In Canada about 14 people live on every 2 square miles of land. About how many people would live on 10 square miles of land?

  F 80

  G 60

  H 70

  J 50

7 The chart below shows some people's weight gain last week.

Weight Gain

Name	Weight Gain Pounds
Sylvia	0.30
Mel	0.75
Etta	$\dfrac{6}{20}$
Herm	$\dfrac{20}{100}$

Who gained the same amount of weight last week?

  A Sylvia and Etta

  B Mel and Etta

  C Herm and Sylvia

  D Herm and Mel

Applied Math

8 A 3-inch line on a diagram of a backyard represents 12 feet. What scale was used to draw the diagram of the backyard?

F 1 inch = 3 feet

G 1 inch = 5 feet

H 1 inch = 4 feet

J 1 inch = 2 feet

9 Chocolate candies sell for $5.60 a dozen. Sales tax is 7%. What is the total cost for 2 dozen candies?

A $0.78

B $11.98

C $5.99

D $12.95

10 Adult polar bears may weigh as much as 1600 pounds. In a year when food is scarce, they may weigh 20% less than normal. If food is scarce, how much would be the combined weight of 5 polar bears?

F 7200 pounds

G 8000 pounds

H 6400 pounds

J 5200 pounds

11 Which percent is equal to 3/4?

A 75%

B 15%

C 25%

D 50%

12 A basketball team won 60 of its 80 games. What percentage of its games did the team lose?

F 50%

G 25%

H 20%

J 60%

Study this bookstore sign. Then do numbers 13 and 14.

This week only!
All books $4
10% discount on
10 books or more

13 The books are on sale for 20% off the full price. Which of these is the best estimate of the regular price of the books?

A $8.00

B $10.00

C $5.00

D $9.00

14 If you buy 10 books, how much money will you save?

F $4.00

G $3.00

H $5.00

J $8.00

Check your answers on pages 117–118.

Lesson 10 Graphs

You see graphs in newspapers or magazines every day. Graphs give the reader a quick understanding of a set of numbers.

Example **On which two days were the dollar amounts of sales the same?**

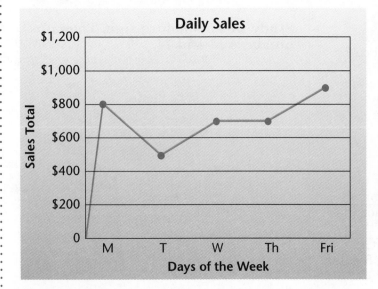

Step 1. Look at the graph. The left-hand side of the graph (total sales in dollars) is called the vertical axis because it starts at the bottom corner and points up. The bottom of the graph (days of the week) is called the horizontal axis because it starts at the bottom corner and points across to the right.

Step 2. Because you are looking for two days on which sales were the same, look for two points of the same height. Check along the vertical axis to make sure the sales totals are the same. Look along the horizontal axis to find the days on which sales were the same.

Sales were the same on Wednesday and Thursday.

Test Example

Read the question. Circle the answer.

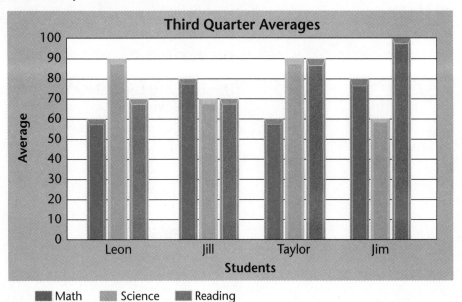

1 Which student had the smallest difference between his or her best and worst average?

A Jim

B Leon

C Taylor

D Jill

1   D There was a difference of 10 points in Jill's best and worst subjects. Leon and Taylor each had a 30-point difference, and there was a 40-point difference for Jim.

Practice

Read the question. Circle the answer.

This graph shows men's and women's college sports participation from 1991 through 1994. Study the graph. Then do numbers 1 and 2.

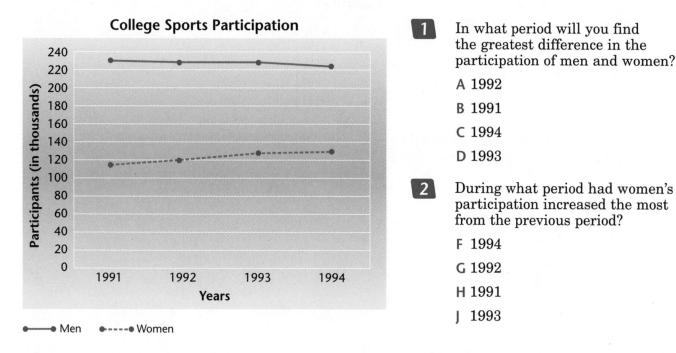

College Sports Participation

●——● Men   ●----● Women

1 In what period will you find the greatest difference in the participation of men and women?

A 1992

B 1991

C 1994

D 1993

2 During what period had women's participation increased the most from the previous period?

F 1994

G 1992

H 1991

J 1993

This graph shows the percentage of income spent on different categories of expenses by different age groups. Study the graph. Then do numbers 3 and 4.

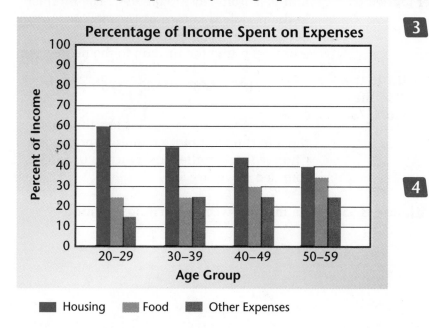

Percentage of Income Spent on Expenses

■ Housing   ■ Food   ■ Other Expenses

3 Which age group uses the largest percentage of its income for housing?

A 50–59

B 40–49

C 20–29

D 30–39

4 Which age group spends approximately half as much for food as it does for housing?

F 30–39   H 50–59

G 20–29   J 40–49

Check your answers on page 118.

Lesson 11 — Probability and Statistics

An average is a number that best represents all the numbers in a group. You probably come in contact with averages every day: a bowling average or the average income of a particular job. A median is a type of average. It is the number that falls exactly in the middle of a set of numbers when the numbers are arranged in order of least to greatest.

Example The weekly earnings of five people are shown in the chart. What is the best estimate of their average weekly earnings? What is the best estimate of the median earnings?

Earnings

Carlos	$759
Loretta	$197
Andy	$553
Marcia	$905
Darryl	$431

Step 1. Find the average. First add the numbers in the list. Regroup as needed.

$$\begin{array}{r} {}^{22}\\ \$759 \\ \$197 \\ \$553 \\ \$905 \\ +\ \$431 \\ \hline \$2845 \end{array}$$

Step 2. Next count the number in the list and divide the sum by that amount. There are 5 numbers in the list, so divide $2845 by 5. $569 is the average weekly income.

$$\begin{array}{r} 569 \\ 5\,\overline{)2845} \\ -25 \\ \hline 34 \\ -30 \\ \hline 45 \\ -45 \\ \hline \end{array}$$

Step 3. Because the question asks for the best "estimate," round the answer to the nearest ten.

$569

9 is greater than 5, so add 1 to the 6 in the tens' place and change the 9 in the ones' place to 0. $569 is rounded up to $570.

Step 4. To find the median, arrange the numbers from least to greatest. The number in the middle is known as the median. Because the problem asks for the best estimate, round the median to the nearest ten.

$197 $431 $553 $759 $905

3 is less than 5, so the 5 in the tens' place remains unchanged. Change the 3 in the tens' place to 0. $553 is rounded down to $550.

The average weekly earnings estimate is $570. The median weekly earnings estimate is $550.

Applied Math

Study the chart. Then do number 1.

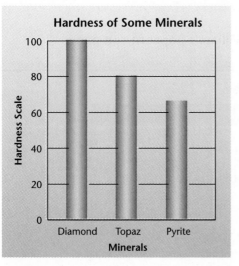

1 What is the best estimate of the average hardness of these minerals?

A   80

B   70

C   100

D   10060

Count how many numbers you add together to determine what to divide by.

1 **A** Add 100 + 80 + 63 = 243. You have 3 minerals, so you will divide by 3. 243 ÷ 3 = 81. 81 rounded down to the nearest ten is 80.

Practice

This graph shows the countries supplying the most oil to the United States. Study the graph. Then do number 1.

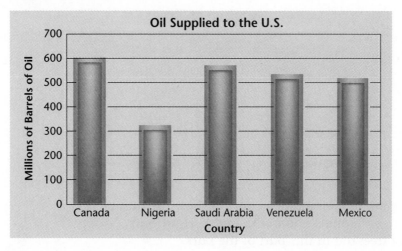

1 Which of these is the best estimate of the median amount of oil supplied by the five countries?

A 300 million barrels

B 400 million barrels

C 600 million barrels

D 500 million barrels

Check your answers on page 118.

Charts

William made a chart to show the annual sales of his company. The chart made it easy for his staff to read and compare the sales. Learning how to read charts can help you solve many types of problems on the TABE.

Example The chart below show the annual sales of William's popcorn company. What were his company's sales in 1990?

Yearly Sales

Year	Sales
1985	← $137,000 →
1990	← $140,000 →
1995	← $129,000 →
2000	← $1,000,000 →

Step 1. Read the question carefully to make sure you understand what information you are looking for. In this example you are looking for the **sales** in **1990**.

Step 2. Find the information that answers the question. Use the correct column and row. Look in the column labeled *Year*. Find 1990. Look at the sales number to the right of 1990.

The sales of this company in 1990 were $140,000.

Test Example

Read the question. Circle the answer.

Number of Trees

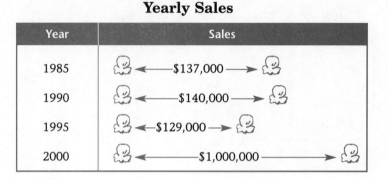

Tree Type	How Many
Sugar Maple	← 15 →
Sycamore	← 17 →
Black Oak	← 10 →
Basswood	← 8 →

1 Hank, a park ranger, made a chart to show the number of types of trees in one section of the park. How many sycamore trees are in this part of the park?

A 10   C 17

B 15   D 8

1 C This section of the park has 17 sycamore trees.

Read the question. Circle the answer.

This chart shows the grams of fiber in a 1-cup serving of several types of grains. Study the chart. Then do number 1.

Fiber Content in 1-Cup Serving

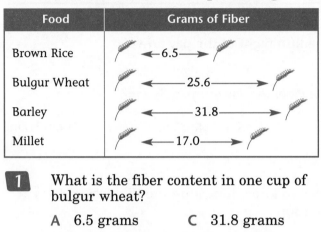

Food	Grams of Fiber
Brown Rice	←6.5→
Bulgur Wheat	←25.6→
Barley	←31.8→
Millet	←17.0→

1 What is the fiber content in one cup of bulgur wheat?

A 6.5 grams   C 31.8 grams

B 25.6 grams   D 17.0 grams

The chart shows the number of restaurants in certain towns in Kansas. Study the chart. Then do numbers 2 and 3.

Kansas Restaurants

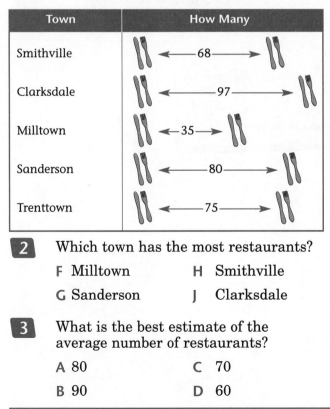

Town	How Many
Smithville	←68→
Clarksdale	←97→
Milltown	←35→
Sanderson	←80→
Trenttown	←75→

2 Which town has the most restaurants?

F Milltown   H Smithville

G Sanderson   J Clarksdale

3 What is the best estimate of the average number of restaurants?

A 80   C 70

B 90   D 60

Jackie made a chart to show the number of points scored by some hockey teams. Study the chart. Then do numbers 4 through 6.

Hockey Points

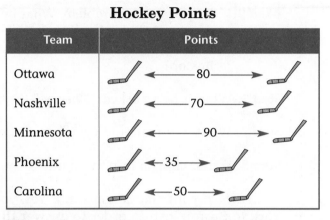

Team	Points
Ottawa	←80→
Nashville	←70→
Minnesota	←90→
Phoenix	←35→
Carolina	←50→

4 How many points has Nashville scored?

F 80

G 60

H 70

J 50

5 How many total points have the top two teams scored?

A 120 points

B 165 points

C 115 points

D 170 points

6 Which statement about the chart is true?

F Ottawa had a much better season last year.

G Phoenix will score 65 more points this season.

H Nashville must score twenty more points to catch Ottawa.

J Minnesota is twenty points ahead of Nashville.

Check your answers on page 118.

Chuck is in charge of setting up the tables for his club's dinner. Each table can seat 12 people. He wants to set up the tables the night before the dinner. How many tables will he need? Before Chuck can set up the correct number of tables, he needs to know how many people will be attending the dinner. Before you can solve problems, you may need to find missing information. Once you have all your information, you can make a plan to find a solution.

Example **Read the word problem. What information do you need to answer the question? Flights leave New York every 45 minutes to fly to Boston. If the first flight is at 6:00 a.m., when will the fifth flight of the day arrive in Boston?**

Step 1. What is being asked? *When will the fifth flight of the day arrive in Boston?*

Step 2. What information do you have? *Flights leave every 45 minutes. The first flight is at 6:00 a.m.*

Step 3. Is that enough information to answer the question? *No.*

Is there is any information missing? **Yes, you need to know how long the flight from New York to Boston lasts in order to answer the question.**

Test Example

A new apartment complex has 10 buildings. What information is needed to find the maximum number of apartments that can be rented?

  A   the number of empty apartments

  B   the number of people who want to rent

  C   the number of apartments in each building

  D   the number of floors in each building

Hint

What is the question? Which facts are needed to solve the problem?

1 C You know there are 10 buildings. You need to know how many apartments are in each building before you can find the maximum number of apartments that are available to rent.

TABE Strategy

Sometimes word problems have extra information that you don't need to solve the problem. Read word problems carefully to decide what information is necessary to solve the problem.

Read the question. Circle the answer.

1 A basketball arena has 65 rows of seats. What information is needed to find the number of people the arena can seat?

A number of people at each game

B number of empty seats per game

C number of seats in each row

D number of rows in each section

2 There are 5 performances of a play at the Civic Center. An equal number of tickets were sold to each performance. What information is needed to find out how many tickets were sold for each?

F the total number sold

G the time of the performance

H the number of performances a day

J the location of the Civic Center

3 This chart shows two of the tallest buildings in the world. If you added the Sears Tower, which information would you need to find the average height of the 3 buildings?

Building	Height
Petronas Tower I	1483 feet
CN Tower	1804 feet

A height of the Sears Tower

B number of stories in CN Tower

C year the Petronas Tower was built

D height of CN Tower

4 Tony wanted to buy hamburger buns and 3 pounds of hamburger meat. The meat cost $2.69 per pound, and a package of buns cost even more. To find the total Tony spent, which information do you need?

F the cost of the meat

G the amount of meat Tony bought

H the cost of the buns

J the distance to the grocery store

5 The planet Neptune has 8 known moons. Pluto has 1 known moon. Saturn has many more known moons. What information is needed to find out how many moons the 3 planets have in all?

A Saturn's distance from the Sun

B time each moon takes to orbit Saturn

C the number of Saturn's known moons

D the names of the Neptune's moons

6 In 1999 638,000 refugees entered the United States. Fewer refugees entered Canada the same year. What information is needed to find how many refugees entered both countries?

F the population of Canada

G how many refugees entered Canada

H the year of the statistic

J countries the refugees came from

7 Ted wanted to buy 14-inch pizzas for his friends. Each of his friends will eat 2 slices. What information is needed to find the number of pizzas Ted will order?

A how many slices each friend will eat

B the number of Ted's friends

C how the pizza is cut

D the size of the pizza

8 Tim made a phone call that cost $2.50 for the first minute and $0.25 for each additional minute. Which information is needed to find the cost of the call?

F the number of phone calls he made

G how long he was on the phone

H how long he has owned the phone

J the time of day the call was made

Check your answers on page 118.

Solve. Circle the answer.

1 A boy read 25 books. What information is needed to find how long it took him to read the books?

   A how long it took him to read each book

   B the number of pages in each book

   C how long it took him to read five books

   D the number of chapters in each book

2 What is the median of the following numbers?

   30 40 60 65 90

   F 90

   G 40

   H 60

   J 65

This graph shows the operating expenses for Mark's business over the last 5 years. Study the graph. Then do numbers 3 through 6.

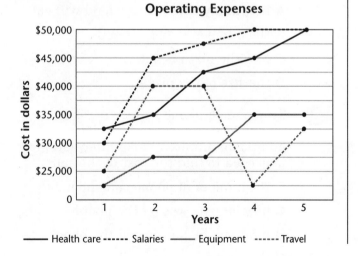

Operating Expenses

3 According to the graph, which expense can Mark expect to increase the most from the fifth to sixth year?

   A travel

   B health care

   C equipment

   D salaries

4 Which of these is the best estimate for the total operating costs for the second year?

   F $35,000

   G $64,500

   H $150,000

   J $37,500

5 In year 4, expenses from least to greatest are

   F salaries, equipment, health care, travel

   G travel, equipment, health care, salaries

   H salaries, health care, equipment, travel

   J health care, health care, travel

6 Which expense is less in the fourth year than it was in the second year?

   A health care

   B travel

   C salaries

   D equipment

7 Wayne wanted to grill two pieces of chicken for his friends. He drove to the grocery store at 5:00 p.m. The chicken cost $2.69 per pound. If you wanted to find how much Wayne spent, which information is needed?

A the number of pieces of chicken his friends ate

B the number of friends

C the number of pounds of chicken he bought

D the time he drove grocery store

8 The chart shows the money collected during a 7-hour book sale. Which of these is the best estimate of the average amount of money collected each hour?

Money Collected

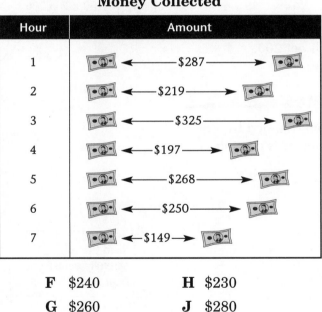

Hour	Amount
1	$287
2	$219
3	$325
4	$197
5	$268
6	$250
7	$149

F $240   **H** $230

G $260   **J** $280

9 The price of a television is $400. When the 4% sales tax is added to this price, what is the total cost of the television?

A $420

B $416

C $412

D $425

10 The school theater has 45 rows of seats. What information is needed to find the maximum number of people the school theater can seat?

F number of rows in each section

G number of seats in each row

H number of people at the show

J number of empty seats at the show

This chart shows some of Canada's imports. Study the chart. Then do numbers 11 and 12.

Canada's Imports

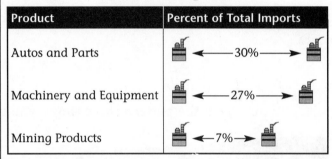

Product	Percent of Total Imports
Autos and Parts	30%
Machinery and Equipment	27%
Mining Products	7%

11 Which of these statements is supported by the information in the table?

A Mining products make up the smallest percentage of imports.

B Mining products make up $\frac{1}{3}$ of all of Canada's imports.

C Autos and Parts make up the smallest percentage of Canada's imports.

D Machinery and Equipment is the most important import of Canada.

12 What percentage of Canada's imports is represented in this chart?

F 62%   **H** 58%

G 64%   **J** 39%

Check your answers on page 118

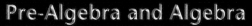

Lesson 14 Functions and Patterns

You see patterns all around you in quilts, tile floors, and brick patios. When someone makes a quilt or lays tile or brick, they follow a pattern to get a particular result. When a shape, color, or number is repeated in a certain order, a pattern is created. Recognizing patterns is one way of solving some problems on the TABE.

Example Begin with 5, then add 4 to that number. Next, multiply that answer by 2. If you repeat the pattern 3 more times, what number will you get?

Step 1. Recognize the pattern that is being followed. The pattern is to add 4, then multiply the result by 2.

Step 2. Set up a table using 5 as the starting number. Repeat the pattern 3 more times.

Number	Add 4	Multiply by 2
5	5 + 4 = 9	9 × 2 = 18
18	18 + 4 = 22	22 × 2 = 44
44	44 + 4 = 48	48 × 2 = 96
96	96 + 4 = 100	100 × 2 = **200**

If you repeat the pattern three times, you will get 200.

Test Example

The table shows "Input" numbers that have been changed to "Output" numbers by following a rule. What number is missing from the table?

Rule: Divide by 2, then subtract 2.

Input	Output
64	30
60	28
24	
10	3

Hint

Read the rule carefully before you begin.

A 16   C 12

B 8   D 10

1 D The rule is to divide each "Input" number by 2 and then subtract 2. If the "Input" number is 24, then 24 ÷ 2 = 12; 12 − 2 = 10.

Read the question. Circle the answer.

1 Sarah can seal 6 envelopes in 20 seconds. How many envelopes would you predict she could seal in 60 seconds?

A 20

B 60

C 18

D 24

2 If you start with 2, multiply that number by 3, then keep multiplying the answer you get each time by 3, you will never get this number

F   52

G   18

H 162

J   54

3 The table shows "Input" numbers that have been changed by a certain rule to get "Output" numbers. What number is missing from the table?

Input	5	15	25	40	50
Output	1	3	5		10

A 5

B 4

C 9

D 8

4 Sound can travel about 700 meters every 2 seconds. How far can sound travel in 10 seconds?

F 4000 meters

G 1750 meters

H 3500 meters

J 7000 meters

5 The table shows "Input" numbers that have been changed to "Output" numbers by applying a specific rule. What number is missing from the table?

Rule: Multiply by 4, then subtract 2.

Input	Output
3	10
6	
8	30
9	34

A 22   C   20

B 24   D   26

This graph shows the number of passenger miles traveled, in billions of miles, by automobiles from 1940 to 1980. Study the graph. Then do number 6.

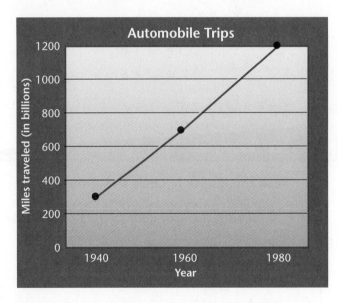

6 If the pattern continues, how many billions of passenger miles would be traveled in 2000?

F 2200   H   2000

G 1800   J   1700

Check your answers on page 118.

Some problems on TABE will have a number sentences with a box to show that a number is missing. For example, you might see a number sentence like $5 \times 6 \times \square = 210$. Finding the missing number is easy if you remember to move the numbers and change the operation sign. You will find several problems with a missing number on the TABE.

Example Solve for the missing number: $5 \times 6 \times \square = 210$.

Step 1. First move 5 to the other side of the equal sign and rewrite the number sentence. When a number is moved from one side of the equal sign to the other, the operation sign is changed to its opposite operation. The opposite operation of multiplication is division. Divide 210 by 5 = 42.

$$5 \times 6 \times \square = 210$$
$$6 \times \square = 210 \div 5$$
$$6 \times \square = 42$$

Step 2. Now move the 6 to the other side of the equal sign. Rewrite the number sentence, change the operation sign, and divide.

$$5 \times 6 \times \square = 210$$
$$6 \times \square = 42$$
$$\square = 42 \div 6$$

Step 3. You can find the missing number by dividing 6 into 42.

$$5 \times 6 \times \square = 210$$
$$6 \times \square = 42$$
$$\square = 42 \div 6$$
$$7 = 42 \div 6$$

$5 \times 6 \times \boxed{7} = 210$.

Step 4. Check your answer by putting the answer in the box in the number sentence then solving.

$$5 \times 6 \times 7 = 210$$

Test Example

Read the question. Circle the answer.

1   What number goes in the box to make the number sentence true?

$3 \times 2 \times \square = 18$

A   2

B   6

C   3

D   4

> **1 C** $3 \times 2 \times \square = 18$
> $2 \times \square = 18 \div 3 = 6$
> $2 \times \square = 6$
> $\square = 6 \div 2$
> $\square = 3$

Read the question. Circle the answer.

1 What number goes in the box to make the number sentence true?

$4 \times \square \times 3 = 60$

A 3

B 2

C 6

D 5

2 What number goes in the box to make this number sentence true?

$5 \times 2 \times \square = 50$

F 4

G 10

H 5

J 6

3 Tran's recipe for lemonade uses 2 parts lemon juice to 5 parts water. How much lemon juice will he need if he uses 15 parts water?

A 3

B 10

C 2

D 6

4 What number makes the number sentence true?

$4 \times \square \times 2 = 16$

F 4

G 6

H 5

J 2

5 If you start with the number 5, then multiply that number by 2 and keep multiplying the result each time by 2, you will <u>never</u> get the number

A 20   C 80

B 30   D 320

6 What number will make this number sentence true?

$2 \times 15 \times \square = 90$

F 3

G 15

H 5

J 9

7 The table below shows record high temperatures for several states. The total is supposed to be 442. Florida's record high temperature is missing. Find the missing temperature.

Record High Temperatures

State	High temperatures
Hawaii	100
Florida	
Oregon	119
Minnesota	114

A 115

B 102

C 119

D 109

8 How many fractions in the box are less than 1?

$$\frac{5}{6}, \frac{8}{7}, \frac{3}{4}, \frac{2}{3}, \frac{10}{3}$$

F 1

G 2

H 3

J 4

Check your answers on page 118.

Lesson 16 · Number Sentences

The first step in solving some problems is to write a number sentence. On the TABE some questions describe a situation and you must choose the correct number sentence to solve the problem.

Example Each year of a dog's life equals about the same as 7 "human years." A 6-year-old dog has lived 42 "human years." What number sentence could you write to find how many "human years" an 8-year-old dog has lived?

Step 1. What question do you need to answer?

How do you find the number of "human years" an 8-year-old dog has lived?

Step 2. What are the key facts needed to answer the question?

The dog has lived 8 years. Each dog year is equal to 7 "human years."

Step 3. What operation will you use to solve the problem?

Multiplication.

8 dog years $\times$ 7 "human years" = $\square$

$8 \times 7 = 56$. **The dog has lived 56 "human years."**

Test Example

Read the question. Circle the answer.

1 A coyote can travel 43 miles in an hour. Which of these number sentences shows how to find the number of miles a coyote can run in 3 hours?

A $43 \div 3 = \square$

B $43 + 3 = \square$

C $43 \times 3 = \square$

D $43 - 3 = \square$

Hint

Think of the steps involved in writing a number sentence: question, key facts, operation.

1 **C** You know how far a coyote can travel in one hour. You need to know how far the coyote can travel in 3 hours. You would use multiplication to find the answer.

Applied Math

Read the question. Circle the answer.

1 Jean read 35 pages of her book in an hour. Which of these number sentences shows how to find the number of pages she can read in 3 hours?

A $35 + 3 = \square$

B $35 \times 3 = \square$

C $35 - 3 = \square$

D $35 \div 3 = \square$

2 Ed had 13 pair of socks. He threw out 5 pairs with holes. Which of these number sentences shows how to find how many pair of socks he has left?

F $13 - 5 = \square$

G $13 \div 5 = \square$

H $13 + 5 = \square$

J $13 \times 5 = \square$

3 In 1950, there were 50 bison on the Bar-Q Ranch. In 2001, there were 5 times more bison. Which number sentence can be used to find the number of bison in 2001?

A $50 - 5 = \square$

B $50 + 5 = \square$

C $50 \times 5 = \square$

D $50 \div 5 = \square$

4 Phyllis has 80 pens. She wants to give an equal number to each of her 5 customers. Which number sentence can be used to find the number of pens Phyllis can give each customer?

F $80 \times 5 = \square$

G $80 - 5 = \square$

H $80 + 5 = \square$

J $80 \div 5 = \square$

5 Luisa ran 24 miles in 4 hours. Which of these number sentences shows how to find the average number of miles she ran each hour?

A $24 \div 4 = \square$

B $24 \times 4 = \square$

C $24 + 4 = \square$

D $24 - 4 = \square$

6 Paul is cooking sausages for 6 people. He figures that each person will eat 2. Which of these number sentences shows how to find the number of sausages he needs to cook?

F $6 \times 2 = \square$

G $6 - 2 = \square$

H $6 + 2 = \square$

J $6 \div 2 = \square$

7 Jordanna is baking cookies for 20 people. She wants everyone to have at least 3 cookies. Which number sentence will show how many cookies Jordanna needs to bake?

A $20 \times 3 = \square$

B $20 + 3 = \square$

C $20 \div 3 = \square$

D $20 - 3 = \square$

8 Chuck had $20, and he saved $9 more. Which number sentence shows how much Chuck had in all?

F $\$20 - \$9 = \square$

G $\$20 + \$9 = \square$

H $\$20 \times \$9 = \square$

J $\$20 \div \$9 = \square$

Check your answers on page 119.

Equations are number sentences that may be used to solve problems. In equations, an unknown value is represented by an italic letter, such as n. In equations, parentheses are used to show items that go together. Parentheses are also used to show multiplication instead of using the "×" sign: $(n)(750)$ is the same as n times 750, or $750n$. You will be asked to solve equations on the TABE.

Example **Over three days, a baby slept 16 hours one day, 17 hours the second day, and 15 hours on the third day. Find the average number of hours the baby slept each day.**

Step 1. Choose the letter x to represent the answer you must find, which is the unknown.

Step 2. Show the total number of hours the baby slept each day.

$$16 + 17 + 15$$

Step 3. To find an average, you need to divide the sum, or total, by the number of days (3). Use a letter to represent the unknown. Write out the equation that will be used to solve the problem.

$$\frac{(16 + 17 + 15)}{3} = x$$

Step 4. Solve the problem in parentheses first. Add $16 + 17 + 15 = 48$.

$$\frac{48}{3} = x$$

Step 5. Divide to solve the equation.

$$x = 48 \div 3 = 16$$

The average number of hours the baby sleeps in a day is 16 hours.

Test Example

Read the question. Circle the answer.

1 A movie runs for 94 minutes. There are 5 showings each day. Which equation can be used to show the total time, in hours and minutes, that this movie runs each day? (60 minutes = 1 hour)

A $(94 \div 5) \times 60 = x$

B $(94 \times 60) \div 5 = x$

C $(94 \times 5) \div 60 = x$

D $(94 \times 60) \div 5 = x$

Hint

How do you change minutes into hours? There are 60 minutes in each hour, so divide the number of minutes by 60.

1 **C** By multiplying 94 × 5, you find the total minutes the film is showing each day. By dividing this sum by 60, you change the total minutes into hours and minutes.

Read the question. Circle the answer.

1 Clark can buy 4 pencils for $1.00. He has $5.00 to spend. To find how many pencils he can buy, Clark uses the equation $4 \times 5 = q$. What does the q in the equation represent?

A the number of pencils Clark can buy with $1.00

B the amount of money Clark has

C the amount of money Clark can spend

D the number of pencils Clark can buy

2 In which of these equations is b equal to 20?

F $b + 5 = 25$ H $20 - b = 25$

G $b + 25 = 5$ J $b - 25 = 20$

Barbara earns $1889.75 per month. The table below shows the federal and state deductions that are subtracted from her monthly paycheck. Study the table. Then do number 3.

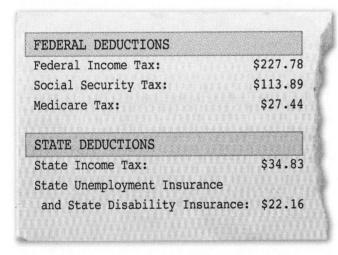

FEDERAL DEDUCTIONS	
Federal Income Tax:	$227.78
Social Security Tax:	$113.89
Medicare Tax:	$27.44

STATE DEDUCTIONS	
State Income Tax:	$34.83
State Unemployment Insurance and State Disability Insurance:	$22.16

3 In which equation is n the total amount of Medicare tax that will be deducted from Barbara's paycheck this year?

A $\dfrac{n}{12} = \$27.44$ C $(n)(\$27.44) = 12$

B $(12)(\$27.44) = n$ D $\dfrac{\$27.44}{12} = n$

4 A basketball team is averaging 8,184 fans per game for an 82-game season. Thirty percent of the fans at each game buy a hot dog. Which equation could you use to estimate how many hot dogs will be sold this season?

F $B = (\text{number of fans per game}) \div 82 \times 0.30$

G $B = (\text{number of fans per game}) + 0.30 \times 82$

H $B = (\text{number of fans per game}) \times 82 \times 0.30$

J $B = (\text{number of fans per game}) \times 82 \times 30$

5 Renee can run 3 miles in 12 minutes. She went running for an hour and used the equation $3 \times 5 = x$ to calculate how far she ran. What does the x represent?

A the number of miles Renee can run in an hour

B the number of miles Renee runs in 12 minutes

C the number of miles Renee can run in 24 minutes

D the number of miles Renee ran this week

6 In Hawaii, the Kilauea Lighthouse is a wonderful spot to watch dolphins, sea turtles, and whales. The $3 admission price is a real bargain! If $4011 was paid for admission last week, which equation can be used to find the average number of visitors to the lighthouse each day?

F $m = (\text{total paid}) \times 3 \times 7$

G $m = (\text{total paid}) \div 3 \div 7$

H $m = (\text{total paid}) \div 3 + 7$

J $m = (\text{total paid}) \times 3 \div 7$

7 In the equation $n - 6 = 32$, $n =$

A 26   C 32

B 38   D 40

Check your answers on page 119.

Lesson 18 Applied Algebra

Equations are used to solve real-life problems on the TABE. Applied Algebra links mathematical ideas to everyday situations.

Example Devon's family ate $\frac{1}{2}$ of a cherry pie, $\frac{1}{4}$ of an apple pie, and $\frac{1}{2}$ of a chocolate pie. How many pies did Devon's family eat?

Step 1. You can solve this problem with addition.

$$\frac{1}{2} + \frac{1}{4} + \frac{1}{2} = g$$

Step 2. Write the equation after you make the denominators of all the fractions the same. Change $\frac{1}{2}$ to the equivalent fraction $\frac{2}{4}$. Rewrite the equation.

$$\frac{2}{4} + \frac{1}{4} + \frac{2}{4} = g$$

Step 3. Add the top numbers to find g.

$$\frac{2}{4} + \frac{1}{4} + \frac{2}{4} = \frac{5}{4}$$

Step 4. Simplify the fraction by dividing the denominator into the numerator.

$$\frac{2}{4} + \frac{1}{4} + \frac{2}{4} = \frac{5}{4} = 1\frac{1}{4}$$

Devon's family ate $1\frac{1}{4}$ pies.

Test Example

Read the question. Circle the answer.

1 Carl read $\frac{4}{8}$ of a book. Patti read $\frac{1}{4}$ of the same book. Carlos also read $\frac{1}{8}$ of the same book. Together, how much of the book did they read?

    A $\frac{7}{8}$

    B 1

    C $\frac{12}{8}$

    D $\frac{10}{20}$

1 A The equation used to solve this problem would be

$$\frac{4}{8} + \frac{1}{4} + \frac{1}{8} = \frac{4}{8} + \frac{2}{8} + \frac{1}{8} = p$$

Together, Carl, Patti, and Carlos read $\frac{7}{8}$ of the book.

Applied Math

Read the question. Circle the answer.

1 Trevor used $\frac{1}{2}$ cup of sugar to make a chocolate cake, $\frac{1}{2}$ cup to make a crumb cake, and $\frac{1}{4}$ cup to make a pineapple cake. How many cups of sugar did he use in all?

A $1\frac{1}{2}$

B $\frac{2}{4}$

C $1\frac{1}{4}$

D 1

2 Kathy's dogs are on a strict diet. She feeds her dog Andy $\frac{7}{8}$ cups of food per day. She feeds Jake $\frac{3}{4}$ cup. And, she feeds Kayla $\frac{1}{4}$ cup. How much food in all does she feed her dogs?

F $1\frac{7}{8}$

G $\frac{11}{16}$

H 2

J 3

3 In his wildflower garden, Patrick wants to use a flower-seed mix containing $\frac{5}{12}$ cup poppy seeds, $\frac{2}{6}$ cup gentian seeds, and $\frac{4}{12}$ cup yarrow seeds. How much seed will Patrick need?

A 2

B $1\frac{1}{12}$

C $\frac{11}{12}$

D $\frac{9}{12}$

4 Clarice used $\frac{2}{3}$ can of stain on her dresser, $\frac{2}{6}$ on her nightstand, and $\frac{5}{6}$ on her bed. How many cans of stain did she use in all?

F 1

G $\frac{9}{15}$

H $1\frac{1}{2}$

J $1\frac{5}{6}$

5 A car was traveling at 60 miles per hour. Another car was traveling 20 miles per hour slower than the first car. At what speed was the second car traveling?

A 40 miles per hour

B 30 miles per hour

C 20 miles per hour

D 80 miles per hour

TABE Strategy

Talk to yourself as you solve word problems. This will help you think through the problem.

Check your answers on page 119.

Solve. Circle the answer.

1 Sasha can buy 3 cookies for $1.00. She has $5.00 to spend. To find how many cookies she can buy, Sasha uses the equation $3 \times 5 = y$. What does the y in the equation represent?

    A the number of cookies she can buy with $3.00

    B the greatest number of cookies she can buy

    C the amount of money she has

    D the amount of money she can spend

2 In the equation $15 + n = 25$, what is n equal to?

    F 30   **H** 10

    G 40   **J** 15

3 Vivian used $\frac{1}{4}$ cup of milk on her cereal, $\frac{1}{2}$ cup of milk with her cookies, and $\frac{3}{4}$ cup of milk for her sister. How many cups of milk did Vivian use in all?

    A $1\frac{1}{2}$ cups

    B 1 cup

    C $1\frac{1}{4}$ cups

    D 2 cups

4 Donuts were on sale at 3 for $2.00. Billy had $8.00 to spend. To find how many donuts he bought, the equation $3 \times 4 = n$ can be used. What does the n in the equation represent?

    F the number of donuts Billy bought

    G the amount of money Billy had

    H the number of donuts Billy bought with $2.00

    J the amount of money Billy spent

5 Donna plays tennis for 2 hours on Monday. She plays tennis for the same amount of time 2 other days each week. Which equation can be used to show the amount of time Donna plays tennis each week?

    A $2 \times 3 = n$

    B $2 + n = 3$

    C $3 - 2 = n$

    D $n \times 2 = 3$

6 In which equation is n equal to 15?

    F $n - 20 = 35$

    G $n + 35 = 15$

    H $n + 10 = 15$

    J $n + 20 = 35$

7 Nina can buy 4 grapefruits for $1.00. She has $3.00 to spend. Nina uses the equation $4 \times 3 = n$. What does n represent?

    A the number of grapefruits Nina can buy with $4.00

    B the greatest number of grapefruits Nina can buy

    C the amount of money Nina has altogether

    D the amount of money Nina can spend on grapefruits

8 A recipe that serves 6 people requires 10 ounces of chicken. In which equation is n the total amount of chicken needed to serve 12 people?

    F $n = \dfrac{10}{6} \times 12$

    G $\dfrac{(n)}{12} = 10$

    H $(12)(6)(10) = n$

    J $\dfrac{(10)(6)}{6} = n$

9 What number goes in the box to make the number sentence true?

$4 \times 2 \times \square = 40$

A 10

B 6

C 5

D 8

10 Vick starts with 7 and multiplies by 2. Then he keeps multiplying the number he gets each time by 2: What number will he <u>never</u> get?

F 28

G 56

H 112

J 49

11 The table shows "Input" numbers that have been changed by a certain rule to get "Output" numbers. What number is missing from the table?

Input	Output
10	5
24	12
44	22
50	

A 10

B 39

C 25

D 2

12 Tony bought 5 blue pens and 3 black pens. He also bought some red pens. If he bought a total of 10 pens, how many red pens did Tony buy?

F 3

G 2

H 5

J 4

13 The first airplane to fly across the Pacific Ocean averaged 89 miles per hour. Which of these number sentences helps you find the number of miles this airplane flew in 6 hours?

A $89 + 6 = \square$

B $89 - 6 = \square$

C $89 \div 6 = \square$

D $89 \times 6 = \square$

14 Nick is planting 5 packets of seeds that contain 20 seeds each. He expects 70% of the seeds to grow into plants. Which equation would you use to find the number of plants Nick can expect to grow?

F $(70 \times 20) \times 0.5 = n$

G $(n \times 20) \times 0.70 = 5$

H $(5 \times 20) \times 0.70 = n$

J $(5 \times 27) \times 0.20 = n$

Check your answers on pages 119–120.

Lesson 19 | Money

You use money every day, so understanding how to solve problems that involve money is important. Some of the questions on the TABE involve money.

Example **Clarise kept her spare money in a shoebox. When she emptied it, she had two $5 bills, three $1 bills, 3 quarters, 2 dimes, and 8 pennies. How much money did Clarise have?**

Step 1. Begin with the highest value of dollars, $5 bills. Find the value of the $5 bills: $5.00 × 2 = $10.00.

Step 2. Find the value of the $1 dollar bills: $1.00 × 3 = $3.00.

Step 3. Begin with the highest value of coins, the quarters. Find the value of the quarters: $0.25 × 3 = $0.75.

Step 4. Find the value of the dimes: $0.10 × 2 = $0.20.

Step 5. Find the value of the pennies: $0.01 × 8 = $0.08.

Step 6. Add to find the total value of the bills and coins.

$$\begin{array}{r} \$10.00 \\ \$3.00 \\ \$0.75 \\ \$0.20 \\ + \$0.08 \\ \hline \$14.03 \end{array}$$

Clarise had $14.03 in the shoebox.

Test Example

Read the question. Circle the answer.

1 Tamika counted $16.79 in her purse. Which is a possible combination of bills and coins she has?

   A two $5 bills, six $1 bills, 2 quarters, 2 dimes, 1 nickel, 4 pennies

   B two $5 bills, six $1 bills, 1 quarter, 2 dimes, 2 nickels, 4 pennies

   C six $5 bills, two $1 dollar bills, 2 quarters, 2 dimes, 4 nickels, 2 pennies

   D six $5 bills, two $1 bills, 2 quarters, 2 dimes, 1 nickel, 4 pennies

TABE Strategy

Eliminate the answers you know are not correct. Choose the correct answer from the remaining options.

1 **A** Find the value of the coins and bills as follows:

$2 \times \$5.00 = 10.00$
$6 \times \$1.00 = \$6.00$
$2 \times \$0.25 = \$0.50$
$2 \times \$0.10 = \$0.20$
$1 \times \$0.05 = \$0.05$
$4 \times \$0.01 = \$0.04$

When you add these, the total is $16.79.

Practice

Read the question. Circle the answer.

1 Which of these is <u>more</u> than enough money to buy a newspaper that costs $0.75?

A 1 quarter, 7 nickels, 1 dime

B 2 quarters, 2 dimes, 15 pennies

C 2 quarters, 1 dime, 2 nickels

D 2 quarters, 1 nickel, 15 pennies

2 It costs $0.15 to produce 1 greeting card. How much does it cost to make 100 cards?

F $1,500.00

G $150.00

H $1.50

J $15.00

3 Alex had three $1 bills, two $10 bills, 2 quarters, 5 dimes, and 6 pennies. How much money did he have?

A $24.06

B $25.16

C $23.16

D $23.06

4 If one share of stock in a company sells for $15.35, how much will 10 shares of stock cost?

F $1,535.00

G $15.35

H $153.50

J $15,350.00

5 Gloria had 4 coins in her pocket. They totaled $0.40, and none of the coins were dimes. Which set of coins could Gloria have had in her pocket?

A 2 nickels, 2 quarters

B 3 nickels, 1 quarter

C 2 quarters, 2 nickels

D 2 dimes, 4 nickels

6 Jake has 3 quarters, 4 dimes, and 3 nickels. Which is the most expensive item Jake can afford?

F a soda for $1.25

G a hamburger for $1.75

H a cookie for $0.75

J a bag of pretzels for $0.99

Check your answers on page 120.

How much time do you have to eat breakfast before you need to leave for work? Do you have time to buy popcorn before the movie starts? Understanding how to add and subtract time will help you answer daily questions and on the TABE.

Example Diana searched the Internet for $1\frac{1}{2}$ hours to find information about housing prices in her area. If she finished her search at 4:05 p.m., at what time did Diana start searching the Internet?

Step 1. Subtract the time spent searching the Internet (1:30) from the time finished (4:05).

$$
\begin{array}{r}
4:05 \\
-\ 1:30 \\
\end{array}
$$

Step 2. Because you can't subtract a larger digit from a smaller, change 4:05 by regrouping. Take 60 minutes (1 hour) from 4 hours to make 3 hours. Then add those 60 minutes to the minutes place. Now subtract.

$$
\begin{array}{r}
3:65 \\
-\ 1:30 \\
\hline
2:35 \\
\end{array}
$$

Diana started searching the Internet at 2:35 p.m.

Test Example

Read the question. Circle the answer.

1 The digital clock displays below shows when Ben started studying and when he finished. How long did Ben study?

started   finished

Hint

There are 60 minutes in an hour.

A 2 hours and 38 minutes

B 3 hours and 48 minutes

C 3 hours and 38 minutes

D 2 hours and 48 minutes

1 **D** Change 7:25 by regrouping. Add 60 minutes to 00:25 and subtract 1 hour from 7:00.

$$
\begin{array}{r}
{}^{6\ 7\,15} \\
7:8\!\!\!/5 \\
-\ 4:37 \\
\hline
2:48 \\
\end{array}
$$

Read the question. Circle the answer.

The Blakey family is driving from Columbus, Ohio, to Des Moines, Iowa by way of Chicago, Illinois. The map shows miles and driving times between cities. The time-zone map shows the four time zones for the continental United States. Study the maps. Then do numbers 1 and 2.

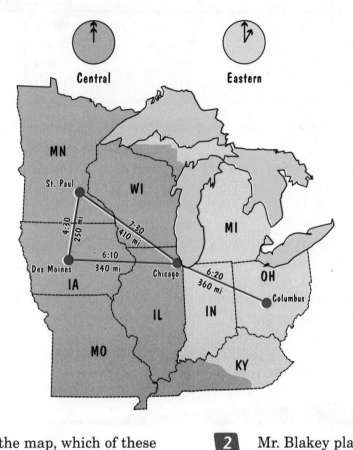

1. According to the map, which of these times is closest to the driving time from Columbus to Des Moines if you travel through Chicago?

A $12\frac{1}{2}$ hours

B $6\frac{1}{2}$ hours

C 17 hours

D 16 hours

2. Mr. Blakey plans to call some friends in Des Moines before the family leaves Columbus. If he calls at 8:30 a.m., what time will it be in Des Moines?

F 6:30 a.m.

G 7:30 a.m.

H 10:30 a.m.

J 9:30 a.m.

Check your answers on page 120.

Length

There are a few basic facts to use when you change yards and feet into meters and back again. In the English system of measurement, 12 inches equal 1 foot and 3 feet equal 1 yard.

Conversion Chart

To change	to	multiply by
feet (12 inches)	meters	0.3048
meters	feet	3.2808
yards (3 feet)	meters	0.9144
meters	yards	1.0936

Example **Melissa long-jumped 10 feet. What are other ways to describe how far Melissa jumped?**

Step 1. You can describe the jump in meters. To change feet to meters, multiply the number of feet (10) by 0.3048.

Step 2. Solve the equation.

$$10 \times 0.3048 = 3.048 \text{ meters}$$

Step 3. The answer is a whole number and a decimal. Round the decimal to the nearest whole number. Since 3 is the whole number, look at the next number to the right (0). The 0 is less than 5, so the whole number 3 remains the same.

Step 4. You could also convert Melissa's jump of 10 feet to inches. Multiply feet times inches: $10 \times 12 = 120$ inches. Or convert Melissa's jump from 10 feet to yards. Divide feet by yards: $10 \div 3 = 3.3$ yards.

Melissa jumped about 3 meters.

Test Example

Read the question. Circle the answer.

1 Which of these shows another way to describe the length of a track that is 440 yards long?

    A   about 750 feet 6 inches

    B   about 12,000 inches

    C   about 400 meters

    D   about 200 feet

1 C $440 \times 0.9144 = 402.336$, or about 400 meters

Read the question. Circle the answer.

1 A wall is 9 feet high. Which of these is another way to describe the height of this wall?

A 3 yards high

B about 2 yards high

C about 60 inches high

D 1 meter high

2 A piece of string was 8 feet long. Which of these is another way to describe the length of the string?

F about 40 meters long

G about 3 meters long

H 2 yards and 2 feet long

J 200 inches long

3 A tree is 23 feet high. Which of these is another way to describe the height of the tree?

A about 250 inches

B about 10 yards

C about 8 meters

D about 7 meters

4 After six weeks, a seedling measured 36 inches tall. Which of these is another way to describe the height of the seedling?

F 1 yard tall

G about 1 foot 4 inches tall

H about 1 yard tall

J about 2 meters tall

TABE Strategy

Rework all incorrect problems with a study partner.

5 Miguel's backyard is 42 feet wide. Which of these is another way to describe the width of Miguel's backyard?

A 10 meters

B about 2 yards

C about 21 meters

D 504 inches

6 The Sears Tower in Chicago is about 484 yards tall. What is the height of this building in feet?

F 1926

G 2808

H 1452

J 1210

7 Jack loves to garden after work. The table below shows the number of hours he spent gardening each day. On which days did he garden more than 1 hour?

Gardening Time

Day	Hours Gardening
Monday	$\frac{7}{6}$
Tuesday	$\frac{6}{7}$
Wednesday	$\frac{3}{2}$
Thursday	$\frac{5}{9}$
Friday	$\frac{9}{10}$

A Wednesday and Friday

B Monday and Wednesday

C Tuesday and Thursday

D Tuesday, Thursday, and Friday

Check your answers on page 120.

Perimeter is the distance around a figure. The length of all the sides are added together to find the perimeter. Some problems on the TABE will involve perimeter.

Example **Pete wanted to find the perimeter of the figure shown below.**

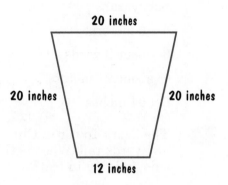

Step 1. Look at the lengths of the four sides.

Step 2. Add to find the perimeter:
20 + 20 + 20 + 12 = 72

The perimeter of the figure is 72 inches.

Test Example

Read the question. Circle the answer.

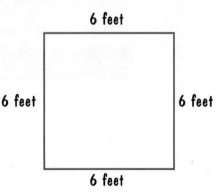

Hint

If all the sides are equal, as in this figure, the perimeter may also be found by multiplying the length of one side by the number of sides.

1 What is the perimeter of this figure?

A 15 feet

B 18 feet

C 24 feet

D 12 feet

1 C The perimeter can be found by adding 6 + 6 + 6 + 6 = 24 feet. You could also multiply 4 sides times the length of each side: 4 × 6 feet = 24 feet.

This diagram shows the dimensions of the Greene's property. Study the diagram. Then do number 1.

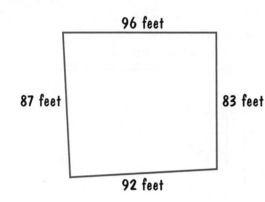

96 feet

87 feet

83 feet

92 feet

1 What is the perimeter of the Greene's property?

A 397 feet

B 346 feet

C 375 feet

D 358 feet

Read the question. Circle the answer.

2 The borders of Colorado form a rectangle. From north to south, it measures about 280 miles. From east to west it measures 360 miles What is the perimeter of Colorado?

F 1280 miles

G 1120 miles

H 720 miles

J 1140 miles

3 A local soccer field measures about 361 feet by about 246 feet. If you ran around the outside of the soccer field, about how far would you run altogether?

A 607 feet

B 1214 feet

C 968 feet

D 853 feet

4 A pie was delivered in a square box that has 6-inch sides. What was the perimeter of the box?

F 12 inches

G 18 inches

H 24 inches

J 16 inches

5 The sides of a triangle are 12 inches, 13 inches, and 20 inches. What is the perimeter of the triangle?

A 57 inches

B 33 inches

C 25 inches

D 45 inches

6 What is the perimeter of this figure?

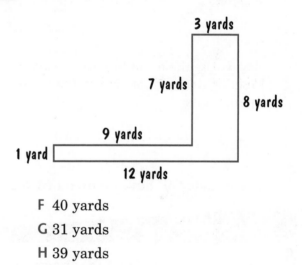

3 yards

7 yards

8 yards

9 yards

1 yard

12 yards

F 40 yards

G 31 yards

H 39 yards

J 50 yards

Check your answers on page 120.

Lesson 23 Area

Understanding how to find area is a useful skill. It will help you buy the right number of cans of paint if you are painting a room. You might also need to find the area of a floor to know how much carpeting to buy.

Example Aleta made the grid shown below to plan a mosaic. The mosaic will measure 12 inches by 12 inches. What will be the area of the mosaic in feet?

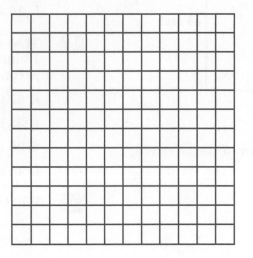

Step 1. Use the formula *Area = length × width* to set up an equation. Express the answer in square units.

$$A = 12 \text{ inches} \times 12 \text{ inches}$$

Step 2. 12 inches = 1 foot. Convert inches to feet.

$$A = 12 \text{ inches} \times 12 \text{ inches}$$
$$= 1 \text{ foot} \times 1 \text{ foot}$$
$$= 1 \text{ square foot}$$

The mosaic will have an area of 1 square foot.

Test Example

Read the question. Circle the answer.

1 The sides of a square are each 24 inches long. What is its area?

   A   24 square feet

   B   4 square feet

   C   24 square inches

   D   4 square inches

Hint

The area of a rectangle is found by using the formula *Area = length × width*. A square is a special type of rectangle.

> **1   B** 24 inches = 2 feet. 2 feet × 2 feet = 4 square feet. A square that has sides each measuring 24 inches has an area of 4 square feet.

Read the question. Circle the answer.

1 A carpet measures 8 feet by 10 feet. What is the area of the carpet?

A 18 square feet

B 80 square feet

C 8 square feet

D 60 square feet

2 For the last census, a town was divided into 2-square-mile sections. The town measures 8 miles by 4 miles. If each person covered one section, how many people were needed?

F 16

G 14

H 18

J 32

3 A carpet has an area of 32 square feet. If the length of the carpet is 96 inches, what is its width?

A 4 feet

B 6 feet

C 2 feet

D 8 feet

4 A board measures 24 inches long and 36 inches wide. What is the area of the board?

F 12 square feet

G 60 square inches

H 84 square inches

J 6 square feet

5 Which of these rectangles has the smallest area?

A 6 ft × 10 ft

B 48 in. × 60 in.

C 9 ft × 7 ft

D 120 in. × 84 in.

6 A bag of grass seed will cover an area of 30 square feet. If Sandra's lawn measures 48 inches by 120 inches, how many bags of seed will she need to buy?

F 1

G 2

H 10

J 13

7 Derrick's car can make one lap around the track in 30 seconds. What information is needed to find out his speed in miles per hour?

A how much gas his tank can hold

B the number of laps he drove

C the type of car he drives

D the size of the track

TABE Strategy

Analyze your mistakes. This will help you avoid repeating them on the TABE.

Check your answers on page 120.

Lesson 24 | Volume and Capacity

More than 10 million households in the United States have pet fish. Whether you need to fill your fish tank, decide how much your refrigerator can hold, or how large of a cabinet you need to buy, knowing how to find volume and capacity is your key to success. Understanding volume and capacity can also help you solve certain problems on the TABE.

Example A refrigerator has a base that is 3 feet wide and 2 feet long. If the refrigerator is 6 feet tall, what is its volume?

Step 1. Volume is found by multiplying length × width × height. It is expressed in cubic units.

Step 2. Set up the equation.

3 feet × 2 feet × 6 feet = x cubic feet

Step 3. Solve the equation.

$3 \times 2 \times 6 = 36$ cubic feet

The volume of the refrigerator is 36 cubic feet.

Example The Lee family must have water delivered to their house while the well is dried up. They have a tank that holds 250 gallons. The water company delivers water in liters. How many liters of water does the tank hold?

Step 1. To find capacity, multiply the known amount by the unit of measurement. In this case, it equals gallons × liters/gallon.

Step 2. Set up the equation.

$250 \times 3.79 = x$ liters/gallon

Step 3. Solve the equation.

$250 \times 3.79 = 947.5$

Hint
1 gallon = 3.79 liters

The water tank holds 947.5 liters.

Test Example

Read the question. Circle the answer.

1 If a container holds 6 pints, how many fluid ounces does it hold?

A 96 fluid ounces

B 22 fluid ounces

C   2.6 fluid ounces

D 10 fluid ounces

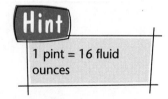

Hint
1 pint = 16 fluid ounces

1 **A** There are 16 fluid ounces in a pint. Multiply 6 pints × 16 fluid ounces/pint = 96 fluid ounces.

Applied Math

Read the question. Circle the answer.

1 A jug holds 5 gallons of water. How many liters of water does the jug hold?

(1 gallon = 3.79 liters)

A 18.95 liters

B 1.31 liters

C 8.79 liters

D 15.79 liters

2 A swimming pool is 18 feet long, 10 feet wide, and 6 feet deep. What is the volume of the swimming pool?

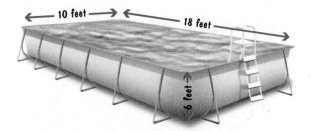

F 180 cubic feet

G 1800 cubic feet

H 1080 cubic feet

J 2010 cubic feet

3 A box is 40 inches long, 15 inches wide, and 12 inches deep. What is the volume of the box?

A 67 cubic inches

B 7200 cubic inches

C 3200 cubic inches

D 600 cubic inches

4 A box is 2 feet wide by 3 feet high. If the volume of the box is 24 cubic feet, what is the length of the box?

F 6 feet

G 3 feet

H 8 feet

J 4 feet

5 Charlie has a storage area that measures 8 feet wide, 12 feet long, and 8 feet high. What is the volume of the storage area?

A 748 cubic feet

B 678 cubic feet

C 768 cubic feet

D 867 cubic feet

6 A milk carton has a width and length of 7 centimeters. If the height of the milk carton is 19 centimeters, what is its volume?

F 49 cubic centimeters

G 931 cubic centimeters

H 856 centimeters

J 133 cubic centimeters

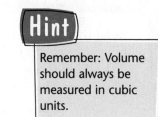

Remember: Volume should always be measured in cubic units.

Check your answers on page 120.

Surface Area

Total surface area of a solid figure is found by adding the areas of each surface. If you know how to find area, you will be able to do problems on the TABE well.

Example **What is the total surface area of the figure below?**

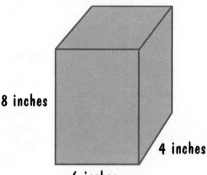

8 inches

4 inches

6 inches

Step 1. Multiply the length × width of each side to find their areas.

The top and bottom are the same, so use 2 × (6 inches × 4 inches) = 48 square inches.

The front and back are the same, so use 2 × (6 inches × 8 inches) = 96 square inches.

The left and right sides are the same, so use 2 × (4 inches × 8 inches) = 64 square inches.

The total surface area of this figure is 208 square inches.

Step 2. Add these surface areas together: 48 square inches + 96 square inches + 64 square inches = 208 square inches.

Test Example

Read the question. Circle the answer.

1 Find the surface area of a figure with a height of 3 feet, a width of 4 feet, and a length of 9 feet.

A   72 square feet

B   160 square feet

C   98 square feet

D   150 square feet

1 D Follow these steps:

2 × (9 × 4) = 72 (top and bottom areas)
2 × (9 × 3) = 54 (front and back areas)
+2 × (3 × 4) = 24 (left and right areas)

The surface area is 150 square feet.

Read the question. Circle the answer.

Daniella built a storage box for blankets, sheets, and towels. This diagram shows the dimensions of the box. Study the diagram. Then do number 1.

1 Daniella wants to cover the inside of the box with lining paper. About how many square feet of lining paper will she need to line the inside of the box, including the lid?

A 60 square feet   **C** 90 square feet

B 86 square feet   **D** 78 square feet

2 What is the surface area of this cereal box?

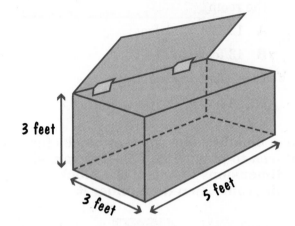

F 1700 square centimeters

G 3000 square centimeters

H 1500 square centimeters

J 140 square centimeters

3 A company is shipping refrigerators. For each refrigerator, they will need a box that has at least 100 square feet of surface area. Which of the following boxes is closest to this requirement?

A width = 3 feet, length = 4 feet, height = 7 feet

B width = 3 feet, length = 4 feet, height = 6 feet

C width = 4 feet, length = 4 feet, height = 6 feet

D width = 3 feet, length = 3 feet, height = 6 feet

4 What is the surface area of a box 4 feet long, 4 feet wide, and 6 feet high?

F 118 square feet   **H** 116 square feet

G 136 square feet   **J** 128 square feet

5 Janet is planning to paint her room, which measures 8 feet high, 11 feet wide, and 15 feet long. If she does not paint the floor, how much surface area will she be painting?

A 706 square feet   **C** 581 square feet

B 686 square feet   **D** 796 square feet

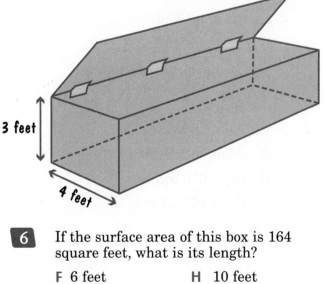

6 If the surface area of this box is 164 square feet, what is its length?

F 6 feet   **H** 10 feet

G 8 feet   **J** 12 feet

Check your answers on page 120.

Solve. Circle the answer.

1 Which answer is exactly enough money to buy a loaf of bread that costs $1.50?

A 4 quarters, 3 dimes, 6 nickels, 5 pennies

B 3 quarters, 4 dimes, 5 nickels, 6 pennies

C 3 quarters, 6 dimes, 4 nickels, 5 pennies

D 3 quarters, 4 dimes, 6 nickels, 5 pennies

2 Ben started jogging at 7:15 a.m. He finished his run at 9:05 a.m. How long did Ben jog?

F 1 hour and 50 minutes

G 1 hour and 40 minutes

H 1 hour and 55 minutes

J 1 hour and 45 minutes

3 One kind of sunflower may grow to 6 feet tall. Which of these is another way to describe the height of the sunflower?

A 3 yards high

B 36 inches high

C 72 inches high

D 1 yard high

4 Akiko put the shot 54 feet. Which of these is another way to describe the distance Akiko put the shot?

F about 180 yards

G about 16.5 meters

H about 670 inches

J about 165 meters

5 A room has an area of 132 square feet. Which of these can be the dimensions of the room?

A 12 feet × 11 feet

B 13 feet × 12 feet

C 11 feet × 11 feet

D 14 feet × 12 feet

Maria bought some wooden blocks for her children to play with. This diagram shows the dimensions of one of the blocks. Study the diagram. Then do number 6.

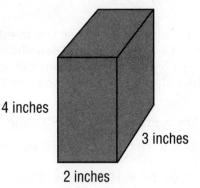

4 inches

3 inches

2 inches

6 What is the surface area of this block?

F 40 square inches

G 64 square inches

H 48 square inches

J 52 square inches

7 Cliff paid for some groceries with a $10 bill. The groceries cost $7.65. Which group of coins could Cliff get back as correct change?

A 5 quarters, 7 dimes, 1 nickel, 5 pennies

B 7 quarters, 5 dimes, 1 nickel, 5 pennies

C 7 quarters, 5 dimes, 5 nickels, 5 pennies

D 7 quarters, 1 dime, 5 nickels, 5 pennies

8 Birgitta began baking cakes for a bake sale at 6:55 a.m. She finished baking at 11:07 a.m. How long did it take to bake all the cakes?

F 4 hours and 21 minutes

G 4 hours and 12 minutes

H 5 hours and 12 minutes

J 5 hours and 21 minutes

Yolanda wants to travel from Philadelphia to Baltimore by bus. Study the bus schedule. Then answer numbers 9 and 10.

BUS SCHEDULE		
Bus Number	Departure Time	Arrival Time
719	7:20 a.m.	10:35 a.m.
823	9:15 a.m.	11:55 a.m.
611	10:40 a.m.	2:00 p.m.
519	1:05 p.m.	3:45 p.m.

9 Which bus is the slowest?

A 611   **C** 823

B 719   **D** 519

10 It takes Yolanda $\frac{1}{2}$ hour to get to the bus station and $\frac{1}{4}$ hour to buy her ticket and get to the departure gate. If she wants to take bus 823, what time should Yolanda leave her house?

F 8:15 a.m.

G 8:45 a.m.

H 8:30 a.m.

J 8:00 a.m.

11 What is the perimeter of a yard that has sides measuring 60 feet, 51 feet, 102 feet, 96 feet?

A 990 feet

B 309 feet

C 390 feet

D 930 feet

12 If a book's front cover measures 9 inches by 12 inches, what is the area of the front cover?

F 81 square inches

G 8 square feet

H 108 square inches

J 21 square feet

13 A fish tank can hold 25 gallons of water. How many liters of water will the fish tank hold?

(1 gallon = 3.79 liters)

A 94.75 liters

B 97.45 liters

C 947.5 liters

D 957.4 liters

Check your answers on page 121.

Lesson 26 Plane Figures

You see many shapes each day: a child's blocks, stop signs, yield signs, a baseball diamond, and so on. Knowing the names of these shapes will help you on the TABE.

Any figure with 4 sides is a quadrilateral. A parallelogram is a quadrilateral in which both pairs of opposite sides are parallel. Parallel lines are lines that always stay the same distance apart.

Example **Kendon was asked to name the following shapes.**

 A 3-sided figure is a **triangle**.

 A **square** has 4 equal sides and is also a parallelogram and a quadrilateral.

A **rectangle** has 4 sides and is also a parallelogram and a quadrilateral.

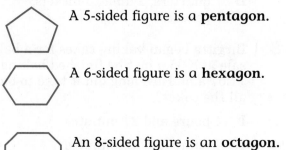

A 5-sided figure is a **pentagon**.

A 6-sided figure is a **hexagon**.

An 8-sided figure is an **octagon**.

Test Example

Read the question. Circle the answer.

1 What shape is shown below?

A hexagon

B octagon

C quadrilateral

D pentagon

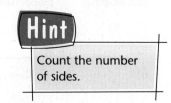
Hint
Count the number of sides.

1 D A 5-sided figure is a pentagon.

Read the question. Circle the answer.

1 What kind of a shape is shown below?

A hexagon

B pentagon

C quadrilateral

D octagon

2 Which of these figures is a parallelogram?

F   G   H   J

3 This famous building is in Washington D.C. What shape is this building?

A octagon

B pentagon

C rhombus

D hexagon

4 Which of the following is a parallelogram?

F triangle

G octagon

H pentagon

J rectangle

5 Which sign has exactly 2 pairs of parallel lines?

A   B   C   D

6 Loretta drew a figure that was a quadrilateral. Which figure did she draw?

F triangle

G pentagon

H square

J octagon

TABE Strategy

If you finish the test early, use the remaining time to check your answers.

Check your answers on page 121.

There are many types of solid figures you will need to identify on the TABE. You may use some of them every day: ice cubes, cereal boxes, basketballs, and so on.

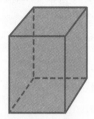

rectangular prism

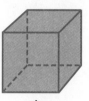

cube

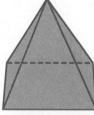

rectangular pyramid

cylinder

cone

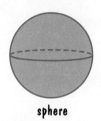

sphere

Example **What shape is a basketball?**

Step 1. Look at the solid figures above.

Step 2. Because a basketball is curved and has no flat surfaces, it must be a sphere.

A basketball is a sphere.

Test Example

Read the question. Circle the answer.

1 What shape is this skyscraper?

A   rectangular prism

B   rectangular pyramid

C   sphere

D   cube

1   **A** Compare the art of this skyscraper to the figures above. This skyscraper is a rectangular prism.

Applied Math

Read the question. Circle the answer.

1 What two solid figures will be formed if the figure is cut along the dotted line?

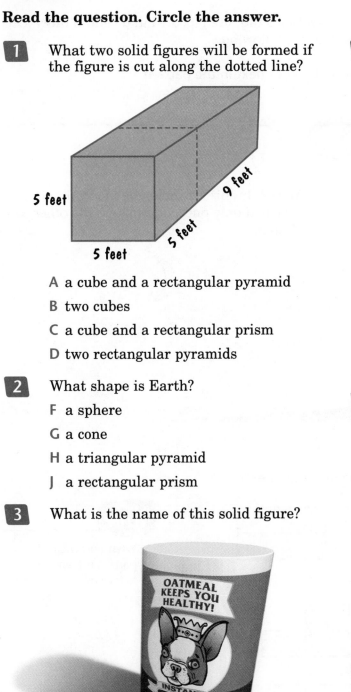

5 feet

9 feet

5 feet

5 feet

A a cube and a rectangular pyramid

B two cubes

C a cube and a rectangular prism

D two rectangular pyramids

2 What shape is Earth?

F a sphere

G a cone

H a triangular pyramid

J a rectangular prism

3 What is the name of this solid figure?

A triangular prism

B cylinder

C rectangular pyramid

D sphere

4 What two solid figures will be formed if the cube is cut along the dotted line?

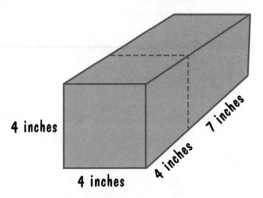

4 inches

7 inches

4 inches

4 inches

F a cube and a rectangular prism

G two rectangular pyramids

H two rectangular prisms

J two square prisms

5 What is a name for the figure?

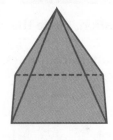

A square prism

B rectangular prism

C rectangular pyramid

D triangular prism

6 What is the difference between a sphere and a cylinder?

F A sphere has two flat surfaces, and a cylinder has none.

G A cylinder is always larger than a sphere.

H A cylinder has two flat surfaces, and a sphere has none.

J The face of a sphere is round, and the face of a cylinder is flat.

Check your answers on page 121.

You learned in Lesson 14 that patterns contain things that are repeated in a certain order. On the TABE you will be asked to solve problems like the following.

Example **Sam was asked to draw the figure that comes next in the pattern shown below.**

Step 1. Ask yourself which pattern is being followed. In this pattern, two figures are repeated.

Step 2. In this example, the moon shape is repeated only once, and follows the other two shapes.

Step 3. If the pattern is continued, **the next figure will be the moon shape.**

Test Example

Read the question. Circle the answer.

1 If the pattern continues, what figure could come next?

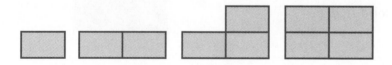

Hint

What numerical pattern is being followed?

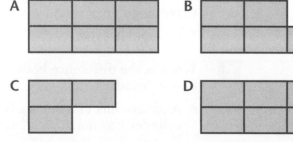

1 **B** In this pattern, each new group has 1 more rectangle than the group before it. Because the last group shown has 4 rectangles, the next group would have 5 rectangles.

Read the question. Circle the answer.

1 If the pattern continues, what figure will come next?

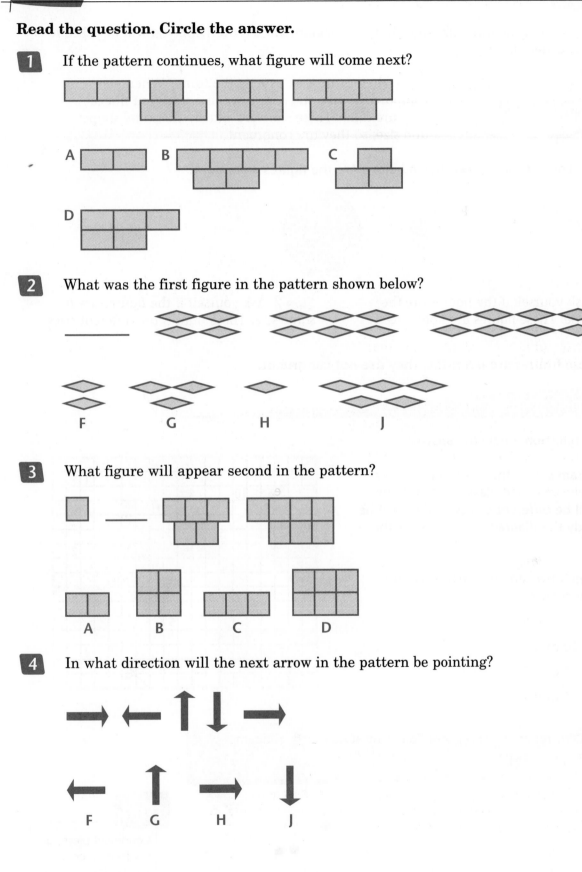

2 What was the first figure in the pattern shown below?

3 What figure will appear second in the pattern?

4 In what direction will the next arrow in the pattern be pointing?

Check your answers on page 121.

Congruency

Figures that are the same size and shape are congruent. On the TABE you will be asked to identify congruent figures.

Do these stars look exactly the same? When you compare the size and shape of these stars you notice they are alike. These stars are exactly the same shape and size, so they are congruent.

Example **Look at the figures shown below. Are the figures congruent?**

Step 1. Ask yourself if the figures are the same shape. These figures are both circles.

Step 2. Ask yourself if the figures are the same size. These figures are different sizes.

Since these figures are not alike, they are <u>not</u> congruent.

Test Example

Read the question. Circle the answer.

This diagram shows the pattern Jasper will use to make a stained glass window. Some pieces will be different colors. Others will be clear. Study the diagram. Then answer the question.

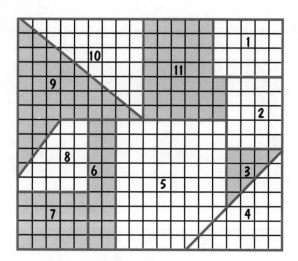

1 Which two stained glass pieces are congruent?

A 7 and 9

B 10 and 4

C 1 and 7

D 5 and 2

1 C Remember that congruent figures must be exactly the same size <u>and</u> shape.

Hint

Congruent pieces do not have to be the same color.

Applied Math

Read the question. Circle the answer.

This diagram shows the garden plan that Meg drew on a piece of paper. Study the diagram. Then do number 1.

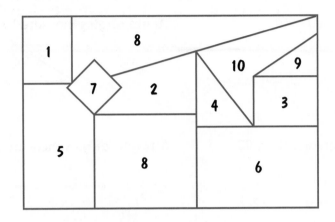

1   Which two sections of the garden are congruent?

A 2 and 4   C   1 and 3

B 5 and 6   D   7 and 9

2   Which pairs of figures are congruent?

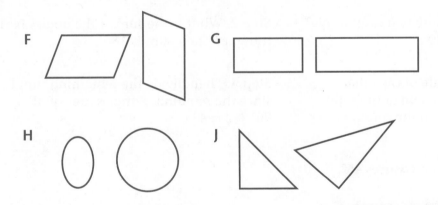

3   Which of the following statements is true about the figure shown below?

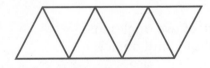

A It contains six congruent triangles.

B Exactly two of the triangles are congruent.

C Exactly four of the triangles are congruent.

D None of the triangles are congruent.

Check your answers on page 121.

Angles are formed by two lines meeting at an endpoint. Angles are written using the symbol "°" or the word "degrees." There are several types of angles. The sum of angles in a triangle is 180°, also written as 180 degrees.

Right angles measure exactly 90°.

Acute angles measure less than 90°.

Obtuse angles measure greater than 90°.

Straight angles measure exactly 180°.

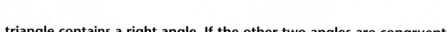

Example **This triangle contains a right angle. If the other two angles are congruent, how many degrees do each of those angles measure?**

Step 1. What is the measure of a right angle? A right angle measures 90°.

Step 2. What is the sum of the angles in a triangle? Their sum is 180°.

Step 3. To find the measure of the other 2 angles, subtract the measure of the right angle from the total sum in the triangle: 180° − 90° = 90°.

Step 4. Then divide the remaining sum by 2 since the remaining angles are equal: 90° ÷ 2 = 45°.

Each of the other angles measures 45°.

Test Example

Read the question. Circle the answer.

1 This diagram shows the measure of two angles in a triangle. What is the measure of the third angle?

   A   125 degrees

   B   86 degrees

   C   68 degrees

   D   98 degrees

   25°   69°

---

1   B   180 − (69 + 25) = 180 − 94 = 86 degrees.

Read the question. Circle the answer.

1 The diagram shows the measure of two of the angles in the triangle. What is the measure of the third angle?

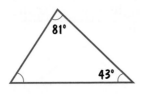

A 56 degrees

B 75 degrees

C 45 degrees

D 47 degrees

2 Jodie's coffee table is triangular in shape. If two of the table's angles measure 36° and 70°, what is the measure of the other angle?

F 94 degrees

G 520 degrees

H 74 degrees

J 254 degrees

3 The diagram shows the measure of two of the angles in the triangle. What is the measure of the third angle?

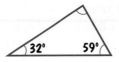

A 91 degrees

B 89 degrees

C 98 degrees

D 88 degrees

4 The triangular stones in a walkway each have two angles that measure 21° and 76°. What is the measure of the third angle?

F 97 degrees

G 83 degrees

H 96 degrees

J 180 degrees

Hint

Some people remember the order of angles from least to greatest with this silly sentence:
Always repair older ships.

<90°	Acute
=90°	Right
>90° and <180°	Obtuse
=180°	Straight

Check your answers on page 121.

Triangles are shapes that have 3 straight lines that are connected. Triangles are classified by shape and by the angles inside. For example, a triangle that has 3 sides that are all the same length and 3 equal angles is called an equilateral triangle. On the TABE you will have to identify different types of triangles.

Equilateral triangle – All the sides and angles are congruent. The interior angles of an equilateral triangle always measures 60°.

Isosceles triangle – Two sides are equal in length.

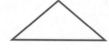

Scalene triangle – No sides are equal.

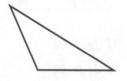

Acute triangle – All the angles are acute.

Obtuse triangle – One angle is obtuse.

Right triangle – One angle is a right angle.

No matter what type of triangle, the sum of the angles of a triangle is always 180°.

Example **What kind of triangle is formed by the shape of the vegetable beds shown below?**

No two sides in these triangles are the same length. They each have a right angle.

They can be described as scalene triangles. They can also be called right triangles.

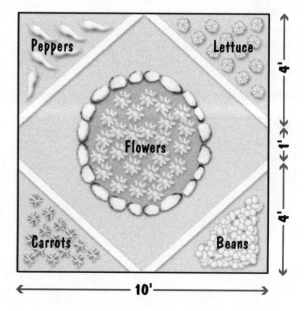

Read the question. Circle the answer.

1 What kind of triangle is formed by the shape of the cabinet in the southwest corner of the room?

    A right triangle

    B obtuse triangle

    C acute triangle

    D equilateral triangle

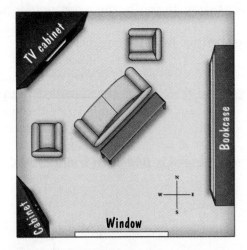

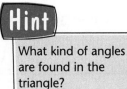

Hint

What kind of angles are found in the triangle?

1 **A** This triangle includes a right angle and no two sides are equal. It is a right triangle.

Practice

Read the question. Circle the answer.

1 What is the measure of angle BCA in the triangle?

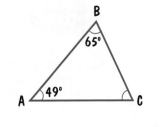

    A 60°   C 66°

    B 90°   D 56°

2 What kind of triangle is shown below?

    F obtuse   H right

    G scalene   J equilateral

The rectangle below has been divided into triangles. Study the diagram. Then do numbers 3 and 4.

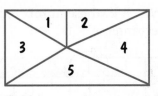

3 How many obtuse triangles are in this figure?

    A 2   C 1

    B 0   D 3

4 Triangle 3 is an equilateral triangle. What is the measure of each of the angles?

    F 90°   H 60°

    G 30°   J 180°

Check your answers on page 121.

Dinner forks and salad forks are similar in shape, but not in size. Two shoes can be similar in design but have different sizes. In math, the word *similar* has a very specific meaning.

These two figures are similar, but not congruent.

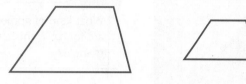

Congruent figures are exactly the same shape and size. **Similar** figures have the same shape. They do not have to be the same size. You may be asked to identify similar figures on the TABE.

Example Which of these figures is similar to triangle ABC?

 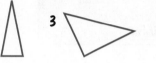  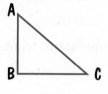

Step 1. Look at triangle ABC.

Step 2. Compare triangle ABC to figures 1, 2, 3, and 4. Determine which figure has the same shape regardless of its size or how it is turned.

Triangle ABC and figure 3 are similar.

Test Example

Read the question. Circle the answer.

1 Which of these numbered rectangles is similar to rectangle ABCD?

Hint

Look carefully at all the figures before you answer.

A 1	C 3
B 2	D 4

1 A Rectangle 1 has the same shape as rectangle ABCD, but it is smaller. The other rectangles are not similar.

Read the question. Circle the answer.

1 Which of these shows figures that are similar but not congruent?

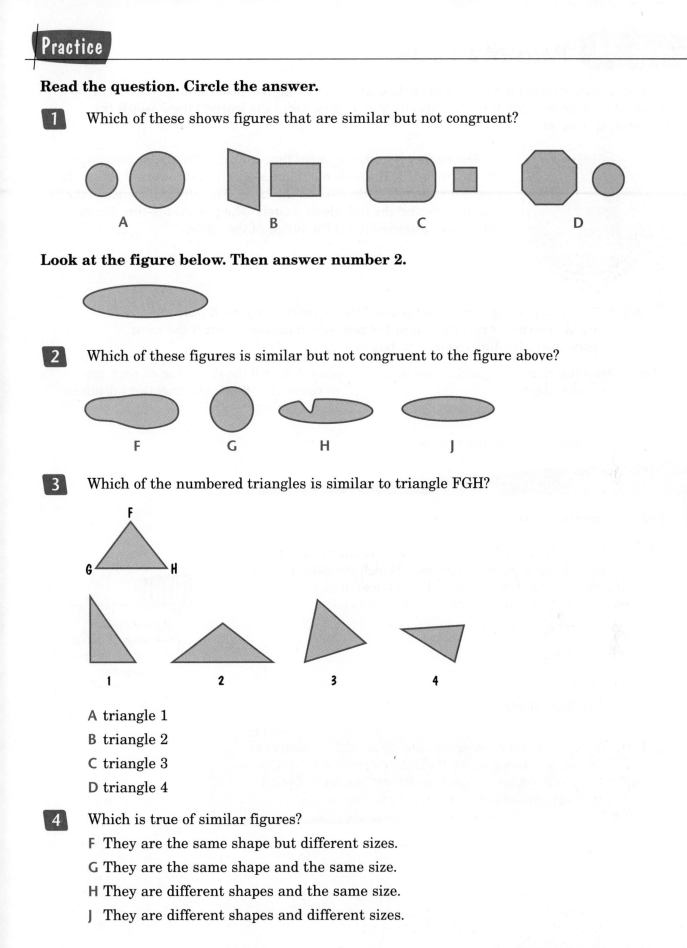

A   B   C   D

Look at the figure below. Then answer number 2.

2 Which of these figures is similar but not congruent to the figure above?

F   G   H   J

3 Which of the numbered triangles is similar to triangle FGH?

1   2   3   4

A triangle 1

B triangle 2

C triangle 3

D triangle 4

4 Which is true of similar figures?

F They are the same shape but different sizes.

G They are the same shape and the same size.

H They are different shapes and the same size.

J They are different shapes and different sizes.

Check your answers on page 121.

Lesson 33 — Parts of a Circle

Joan's teacher asked her to draw a circle and label the diameter and radius. Joan soon realized that circles have their own special vocabulary. Once she learned these words the assignment was easy.

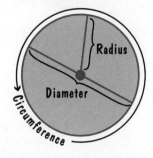

The **radius** is a line segment that connects the center to a point on the circle. The **diameter** is a line segment that passes through the center and has its endpoints on the circle. The **circumference** is the distance around the outside of a circle. The **area** is the number of square units needed to fill the inside of the circle.

Example   Tory is repotting some of his plants into larger round pots. If pots are sized in inches across the top of the pot, which measurement is the most convenient for Tory to know to buy new pots?

Step 1. Read the example question carefully. How are pots measured?

Step 2. Recall the definition of each part of the circle. Which one measures distance across a circle?

Diameter measures the distance across a circle.

Test Example

Read the question. Circle the answer.

1   Malcolm is digging a circular garden. He wants to put in a fence with fence posts every 6 feet. Which measurement is the most convenient for Malcolm to know in order to determine how many fence posts he will need?

   A   the diameter

   B   the radius

   C   the area

   D   the circumference

Hint

Think about the definition of radius, area, circumference, and diameter.

1   **D** The circumference shows the distance around the outside of the circle. Option A names the distance across a circle. Option B names the distance from the center of the circle. Option C names the square units inside the circle.

Read the question. Circle the answer.

1 How would you describe the line shown in the circle below?

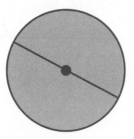

A the area

B the circumference

C the diameter

D the radius

2 If you wanted to know the distance from the center to the outside of the circle, which would be the most convenient measurement to know?

F the area

G the radius

H the perimeter

J the circumference

3 Margie wants to buy a cover for her child's round wading pool. She knows the pool is 48 inches across. Which measurement will be most helpful when she goes to buy the correct size pool cover?

A the radius

B the circumference

C the diameter

D the area

4 Which measurement will give the number of square units needed to cover a circle?

F the radius

G the diameter

H the area

J the center

5 Mr. Saunders wants his soccer team to practice passing the ball to each other. He drew a large circle on the field. He wants his players to stand at equal intervals around the edge of the circle. Which would be the most helpful to figure out how far apart each player should stand?

A the area

B the radius

C the diameter

D the circumference

 **TABE Strategy**

Draw a circle and label its parts to help you answer the questions.

Check your answers on page 121.

Solve. Circle the answer.

1   If the pattern continues, how many figures will come next?

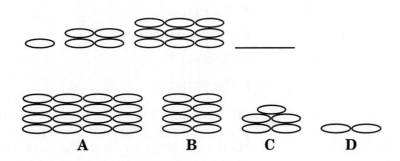

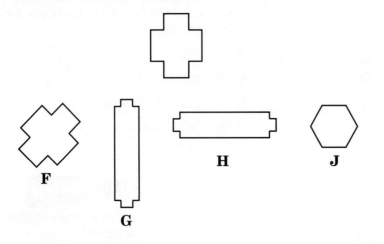

2   Which figure is congruent to the figure shown below?

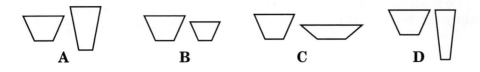

3   Which pair of trapezoids is similar?

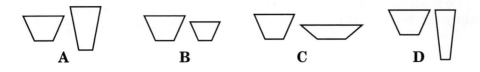

4   Which of these figures is <u>not</u> a parallelogram?

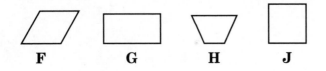

Applied Math

5 What is the measure of the third angle?

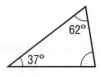

   A 118 degrees

   B   99 degrees

   C   81 degrees

   D 261 degrees

6 What kind of triangle is shown in the shape below?

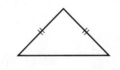

   F obtuse

   G scalene

   H isosceles

   J equilateral

7 Janine wants to cover a circular room with carpeting. Which measurement will be the most convenient to know before she buys carpet?

   A the circumference

   B the radius

   C the area

   D the diameter

8 What kind of triangle is shown in the shape below?

   F equilateral   **H** right

   G acute   **J** scalene

9 What shape is the figure shown below?

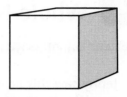

   A rectangular pyramid

   B cube

   C square

   D cylinder

10 What kind of shape is formed by the window of this house?

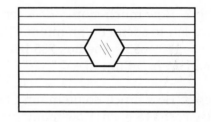

   F hexagon

   G octagon

   H parallelogram

   J quadrilateral

Check your answers on page 122.

Lesson 34 **Whole Numbers in Context**

On the TABE you'll be asked to solve many word problems using whole numbers.

Example **Jenny saw this advertisement for a special sale. Jenny can spend up to $75. If she buys 8 sample CDs, how many premium CDs can she buy?**

To help solve the problem, Jenny asks herself these questions.

Step 1. How much do sample CDs cost? Sample CDs are $5 each. 8 × $5 = $40. She will spend $40 on sample CDs.

Step 2. How much money does Jenny have left to spend on premium CDs? $75 − $40 = $35. She has $35 left to spend on premium CDs.

Step 3. How much do premium CDs cost? They cost $15 each. How many premium CDs can she buy? $35 ÷ 15 = 2 with $5 left over.

Jenny can buy 2 premium CDs and have $5 left over.

CD PRICES

ELECTRONICAREDUX
ONSTAGE AGAIN
Premium CDs
$15.00 each

POLKA!
POLKA!
POLKA!
Discount CDs
$7.00 each

Groove Tunes
Sample CDs
$5.00 each

Test Example

Read the question. Circle the answer.

1 Dan and Angelina want to drive to Monterey, California, from their home in Santa Barbara. The highway route is 246 miles. The scenic route along the ocean is 216 miles. How much farther is it to take the highway route rather than the scenic route?

A 276 miles   C 30 miles

B 132 miles   D 45 miles

1 **C** Subtract 246 (length of the longest route) − 216 (length of the shortest route) = 30 miles more to take the highway route.

Read the question. Circle the answer.

1 Mark wanted to install a fence around his yard. How many 6-foot sections of fencing will be needed to put a fence on the north side of the yard?

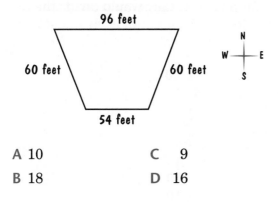

A 10

C 9

B 18

D 16

The Greene family is driving from Miami, Florida, to Atlanta, Georgia. The map below shows the miles they will drive. Study the map. Then do number 2.

Driving Distance Map

2 How many miles will the Greene family drive if they go from Miami to Atlanta through Jacksonville?

F 793 miles

H 820 miles

G 810 miles

J 723 miles

This graph shows the change in temperature in New York City on May 29. Study the graph. Then do numbers 4 and 5.

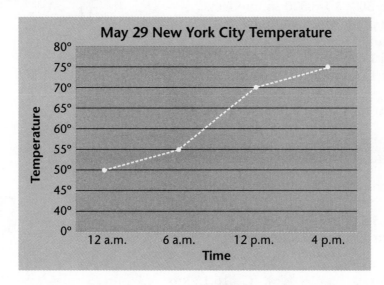

3 What is the difference between the temperature at 12 a.m. and 4 p.m.?

A 15°

C 25°

B 20°

D 10°

4 What is the difference between the temperature at 6 a.m. and 12 p.m.?

F 10°

H 20°

G 25°

J 15°

Check your answers on page 122.

Decimals in Context

Some problems on the TABE will ask you to add, subtract, multiply, and divide decimals.

Example **Dan and Angelina went to dinner. The bill was $40.00, and they decide to leave a $6.50 tip. If they split the bill, how much did each of them pay?**

Step 1. First they would add the tip of $6.50 to the bill of $40.00.

$$\begin{array}{r} \$40.00 \\ + \$6.50 \\ \hline \$46.50 \end{array}$$

Step 2. Next they would divide the total by 2 to find the amount each would pay.

$$\begin{array}{r} 23.25 \\ 2\overline{)46.50} \\ -4 \\ \hline 06 \\ -6 \\ \hline 05 \\ -4 \\ \hline 10 \\ -10 \\ \hline 0 \end{array}$$

Each must have paid $23.25.

Example **Casper is painting his fence. It stands 10 feet tall and is 50 feet long. A can of exterior paint costs $26.70 per gallon. Each gallon will cover 400 square feet. What would be the total cost of the paint needed to paint the fence?**

Step 1. Find the total area that needs to be painted. Remember that you find area by multiplying length × width. The answer will be in square feet. 50 × 10 = 500 square feet. Because 1 can of paint will cover only 400 square feet and Casper needs to cover 500, he will need 1 can for the first 400 square feet of fence and 1 can more to finish.

Step 2. To find the total cost of the paint, multiply the cost of a can times the number of cans needed, which is 2.

$$\begin{array}{r} \overset{1\ 1}{\$26.70} \\ \times\ 2 \\ \hline \$53.40 \end{array}$$

The cost of paint for Casper's fence will be $53.40.

Test Example

Read the question. Circle the answer.

1 Tim rode 15.5 miles on his bicycle to the park yesterday. What is the distance in kilometers that Tim rode to the park?

  A 9.61 km

  B 25 km

  C 16.12 km

  D 14.88 km

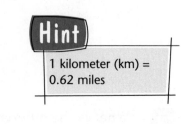

Hint

1 kilometer (km) = 0.62 miles

1 **B** Divide total miles (15.5) by the number of miles in 1 km (0.62). 15.5 ÷ 0.62 = 25

Read the question. Circle the answer.

1 The Brown family is making 10 cakes for a school bake sale. Each cake will contain chocolate chips. One bag of chocolate chips is enough for 2 cakes. If each bag costs $2.99, how much will the chocolate chips cost?

A $11.96

B $17.94

C $8.97

D $14.95

2 Ted ran in a 3.1 mile race. What is the distance in kilometers that Ted ran?

(1 kilometer [km] = 0.62 miles)

F 3.72 km

G 5 km

H 1.922 km

J 2.48 km

Clark kept track of his monthly expenses. The chart shows some of his expenses. Study the chart. Then do numbers 3 and 4.

Monthly Expenses

Rent	$865.75
Electric	$78.16
Entertainment	$49.70
Telephone	$30.95
Apartment Insurance	$61.85

3 Clark earns $1978.64 per month. After deducting all of his expenses listed here, how much does Clark have left to spend?

A $875.90

B $921.56

C $892.23

D $982.32

4 It is 3.7 miles from Keifer's farm into town. How far is the distance in kilometers?

(1 kilometer [km] = 0.62 miles)

F 2.29 km

G 4.32 km

H 5.97 km

J 3.08 km

5 Jack took his wife to a baseball game. Each ticket cost $12.75 and Jack paid with two $20 bills. How much change did Jack receive?

A $27.00

B $14.50

C $25.50

D $12.75

6 Wendy needs 12 windows for her house. Each window will need 10 feet of aluminum to finish it. The aluminum comes in 30-foot rolls. If each roll costs $9.53, how much will the aluminum cost?

F $38.12

G $114.36

H $95.30

J $28.59

Check your answers on page 122.

Lesson 36 Fractions in Context

In each window box Sam planted $\frac{1}{4}$ package of flower seeds. If he has $\frac{3}{4}$ package of flower seeds, he can plant seeds in 3 containers.

Many problems on the TABE involve multiplying and dividing fractions. To multiply like fractions, multiply the numerators of each fraction. Then multiply the denominator.

$$\frac{1}{3} \times \frac{2}{5} = \frac{2}{15}$$

To divide fractions, reverse the numerator and denominator of the second fraction and change the operation sign to multiplication. Then multiply the fractions.

$$\frac{3}{4} \div \frac{1}{4} \text{ becomes } \frac{3}{4} \times \frac{4}{1} = \frac{12}{4} = 3$$

To change a whole number to a fraction, put the whole number over a 1.

$$1 = \frac{1}{1}, \ 4 = \frac{4}{1}, \ 15 = \frac{15}{1}, \text{ and so on.}$$

Example **Ken plans to study for $1\frac{1}{2}$ hours each day for his GED. The test is in 12 days. How many hours will Ken be studying?**

Step 1. Change $1\frac{1}{2}$ to a fraction. Multiply the denominator by the whole number. Add the numerator of the fraction to the result: 2 + 1 = 3. Put this result over the original denominator of the fraction.

Step 2. Multiply by the number of days:

$$\frac{3}{2} \times \frac{12}{1} = \frac{36}{2}$$

Step 3. Simplify the fraction by dividing the numerator by the denominator.

$$36 \div 2 = 18$$

Ken will study for 18 hours.

Test Example

Read the question. Circle the answer.

1 Rosa has 50 pieces of candy. She ate $\frac{1}{10}$ of the candy on the way home from the store. She divides the rest of the candy among 5 people. How many pieces of candy does each person get?

A 8

B 9

C 6

D 7

1 B First multiply 50 by $\frac{1}{10}$ to find how many pieces of candy Rosa ate. $\frac{50}{1} \times \frac{1}{10} = \frac{50}{10}$. Simplify the fraction to $\frac{5}{1}$ or 5. Rosa ate 5 pieces of candy. Then subtract the candy she ate from the total amount of candy: $50 - 5 = 45$. Rosa had 45 pieces left to split among 5 people. Now divide the candy that is left by the number of people: $45 \div 5 = 9$. Each person gets 9 pieces of candy.

Practice

Read the question. Circle the answer.

1 Phil is buying bags of cement to repair his sidewalk. Each bag of cement weighs $23\frac{1}{2}$ pounds. How many pounds of cement will Phil have if he buys 3 bags?

A $69\frac{1}{2}$ pounds   C 68 pounds

B $70\frac{1}{2}$ pounds   D $73\frac{1}{2}$ pounds

Carlos wants to put ceiling tiles in his den. This diagram shows the dimensions of the den. Study the diagram. Then do number 2.

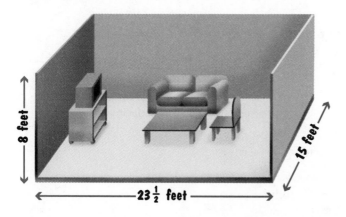

8 feet — 15 feet — $23\frac{1}{2}$ feet

2 Each ceiling tile covers $2\frac{1}{2}$ square feet. What is the minimum number of ceiling tiles Carlos will need to cover the ceiling of his den?

F 200   H 152

G 146   J 141

Cathy is making meatloaf for her family. This list shows the ingredients for a recipe that will serve 4 people. Study the recipe. Then do numbers 3 and 4.

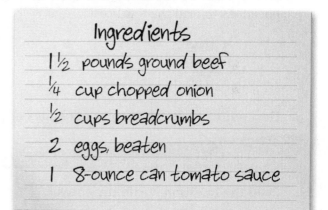

Ingredients
$1\frac{1}{2}$ pounds ground beef
$\frac{1}{4}$ cup chopped onion
$\frac{1}{2}$ cups breadcrumbs
2 eggs, beaten
1 8-ounce can tomato sauce

3 If Cathy wants to double the recipe, how many pounds of ground beef will be needed?

A 4 pounds   C 3 pounds

B $2\frac{1}{2}$ pounds   D $3\frac{1}{2}$ pounds

4 Cathy wants to make a smaller meatloaf for lunch. If she cuts the recipe in half, how much breadcrumbs will Cathy use?

F $\frac{1}{6}$ cup   H $\frac{1}{4}$ cup

G $\frac{2}{3}$ cup   J $\frac{5}{6}$ cup

Check your answers on page 122.

Lesson 37 | Percents in Context

You use percents every day to determine amounts such as discounts and sales tax. Percent means "per hundred." Percents may be used to help solve many problems on the TABE.

Example The sales tax in South County is 8%. If Don bought 2 two super packages of paper towels at $5.00 each, how much did he spend?

Step 1. Multiply the cost of each package by the number of packages purchased: $5.00 × 2 = $10.00.

Step 2. The sales tax is 8%. Remember that 8% is equal to $\frac{8}{100}$, which can be written as the decimal 0.08. Multiply the total cost of the paper towels by 0.08 to find the amount of the tax:

$$\begin{array}{r} \$10.00 \\ \times\ 0.08 \\ \hline .8000 \end{array}$$

Step 3. Add the tax amount to the cost of the packages to find the total cost:

$$\begin{array}{r} \$10.00 \\ +\ 0.80 \\ \hline \$10.80 \end{array}$$

Don paid $10.80 for 2 super packages of paper towels.

Test Example

Read the question. Circle the answer.

1   A store is advertising videos at 80% of the regular price of $12.00. How much is the sale price of each video?

    A $8.00

    B $8.60

    C $9.60

    D $10.00

Hint

Your first step is to change 80% to a decimal.

1   **C**   Change 80% to 0.80. Next multiply this by the regular price of $12.00 to find the sale price: $12.00 × 0.80 = $9.60.

Read the question. Circle the answer.

1 Chuck bought 3 books. Each book costs $15.75. The sales tax is 6%. What is the total cost of the books? (Round to the nearest cent.)

A $50.09

B $50.15

C $50.03

D $50.21

2 In a recent survey of 100,000 people, 25% chose red as their favorite color. How many people chose red as their favorite color?

F   25

G   250

H 25,000

J   2500

The circle graph shows the population of the world. Study the graph. Then do number 3.

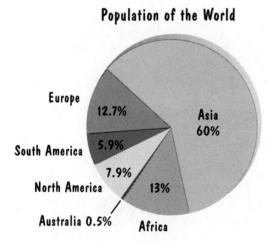

Population of the World

3 According to the graph, what is the total percent of population living in North and South America?

A   23.5%

B   13.8%

C   12.7%

D 138%

4 Jane bought 2 boxes of muffins. Each box costs $3.49. The sales tax is 6%. What is the total cost of the muffins? (Round to the nearest cent.)

F $7.25

G $7.82

H $6.98

J $7.40

5 Of 520 fans at a baseball game, 130 bought souvenir programs. What percentage of fans bought a program?

A 25%

B 15%

C 45%

D 35%

6 About 20% of the atmosphere surrounding Earth is oxygen. What fraction of the Earth's atmosphere is oxygen?

F $\frac{1}{4}$

G $\frac{1}{2}$

H $\frac{1}{5}$

J $\frac{1}{3}$

7 If $\frac{1}{2}$ of a class of 36 students registered for an after-school art club, what percent of students is this?

A 36%

B 50%

C 56%

D 18%

Check your answers on page 122.

Tina was ordering plants from a mail-order nursery. The details below explain the shipping charges. Study the explanation. Then do numbers 1 and 2.

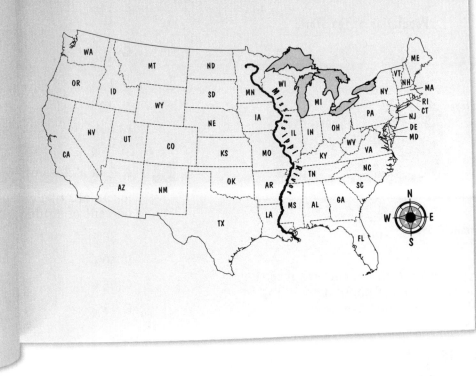

Plant Heaven Mail-Order Nursery | 53

SHIPPING INFORMATION

Zone 1 All states West of the Mississippi River
Add 20% of the total starting with a minimum shipping and handling charge of $5.00.

Zone 2 All states East of the Mississippi River
All plants will be shipped by air. Add 35% of the total starting with a minimum shipping and handling charge of $15.

1 Tina lives in Pennsylvania (PA). If she ordered $80 worth of plants, what is her total cost?

A $118

B $28

C $102

D $108

2 The nursery was running a sale for all orders over $100. There was a 10% discount on the plants, but shipping was not discounted. If Joe wanted $120 worth of plants shipped to his home in Arizona (AZ), how much did he pay?

F $131.80

G $129.60

H $127.90

J $135.00

3 Sheila went for a 9-mile hike. If she wanted to take a break after each $\frac{3}{4}$ of a mile, how many breaks did she take?

A 9

B 12

C 6

D 14

The intensity, or loudness, of sound is measured in decibels. The chart below shows the decibel levels of certain sounds. Study the chart. Then do numbers 4 and 5.

Loudness

Sound	Decibels
Breathing	10
Street traffic	?
Subway	100
Jet Airplane	140

4 The decibel level of street traffic is $\frac{1}{2}$ of the decibel level of a jet airplane. What is the decibel level of a street traffic?

F 7

G 70

H 0.7

J 77

5 A sound with a decibel level 20% greater than the decibel level of a subway can cause pain in the ear. What decibel level would cause discomfort?

A 120 decibels

B 60 decibels

C 140 decibels

D 80 decibels

Check your answers on page 122.

Lesson 38 | **Reasonableness of an Answer**

A reasonable answer is one that makes sense. The numbers fit the situation. If you recognize that an answer isn't reasonable, you know you have to rethink the solution to the problem.

Example **Susan works out with weights. She lifts a 10 pound weight 10 times during each of her workouts. She told her friend, Dawn, that if she worked out 10 days in a row, she would lift a total of 100,000 pounds. Is Susan correct?**

Step 1. Think about the numbers in the problem. 100,000 pounds is a lot of weight to lift in only 10 days.

Step 2. Plan a solution. Ask yourself: How could I figure out how much Susan would have to lift each day for 10 days to reach 100,000 pounds?

Step 3. Do the math. $100,000 \div 10 = 10,000$. Susan would have to lift 10,000 pounds each day to reach 100,000 pounds.

Susan is incorrect. Lifting a 10-pound weight 10 times a day will take 1000 days (about 3 years) to add up to 100,000 pounds.

Example **The trunks of most trees increase by about 1 inch in circumference per year. At this rate, Jordan said it would take a tree about 300 years to increase its trunk size by 1 foot. Is Jordan's answer reasonable?**

Step 1. Think about the numbers in the problem.
- The growth rate is 1 inch per year.
- Jordan is estimating how long it will take for the tree to increase its trunk 1 foot in circumference. There are 12 inches in a foot.
- 300 years is a long time. Not many trees live to this age.

Step 2. Plan a solution. Ask yourself: How could I figure how long it would take for a tree trunk to increase by 1 foot? Multiply the growth rate times the number of inches in a foot.

Step 3. Multiply. 1 inch per year × 12 inches = 12 years

Jordan's answer is not reasonable. 300 years is much too long.

Read the question. Circle the answer.

1 Mike works 20 days a month at his job. If he earns about $80 per day, what is the best estimate of about how much Mike earns in a month?

    A $60,000

    B $16,000

    C $160

    D $1600

Hint

If you simplify a multiplication problem by removing the 0's, don't forget to rewrite them in your answer.

1 D Remove the two 0's to simplify the problem. Multiply $2 \times 8 = 16$. Now rewrite the two 0's to the end of 16, and Mike's monthly earnings are about $1600.

Practice

Read the question. Circle the answer.

1 About 60 families live in the Bermuda Town development. The area of the development is 10 square miles. About how many families are there per square mile?

    A 6000

    B   600

    C   6

    D   60

2 Alex had 10 pieces of lumber for his project. He measured only 3 pieces of lumber. Which of these is the best estimate of the fraction of lumber Alex measured?

    F between $\frac{1}{3}$ and $\frac{1}{2}$

    G between $\frac{1}{4}$ and $\frac{1}{3}$

    H between $\frac{2}{3}$ and $\frac{3}{4}$

    J between $\frac{1}{2}$ and $\frac{2}{3}$

3 Kelli runs about 5 miles round trip to and from the park, 3 days each week. At the end of 20 weeks, what is the best estimate of about how far Kelli had run?

    A   3000 miles

    B   30 miles

    C   300 miles

    D 30,000 miles

4 Jackson needs to place a classified ad in the local newspaper. Each 1-inch space of text costs $4.00 for 14 days. If Jackson has $13.00, about how many inches of text can he buy?

    F   3 inches

    G $3\frac{1}{2}$ inches

    H 56 inches

    J $10\frac{1}{4}$ inches

Check your answers on page 122.

Lesson 39 Rounding

Rounding is an estimation technique. When you round, you replace the numbers in the original problem with compatible numbers to make a simpler problem.

Example Ben plans to refurnish his house. He has $5000.00 to spend. If his plans call for spending $1257.00 on his living room, $675.52 on his bathroom, and $2340.50 on his bedroom, will he have approximately enough money to get what he wants?

Step 1. Round each of the numbers to the nearest hundred. Look for the rounding number—the digit to the right of the place to which you are rounding. If this digit is less than 5, the digit to its left does not change. If this digit is 5 or greater, add 1 to the hundreds place. Change all digits to the right into 0s.

The digit to the right of the hundreds place is in the tens place.

1257.00 rounds to 1300.00. The rounding number is 5 or greater, so the 2 rounds to 3.
675.52 rounds to 700.00. The rounding number is 5 or greater, so the 6 rounds to 7.
2340.50 rounds to 2300.00. The rounding number is less than 5, so the 3 does not change.

Step 2. Add the rounded numbers. 1300 + 700 + 2300 = 4300.

Ben will spend about $4300.00. He will have enough money.

Example Which of these numbers when rounded to the nearest tenth is the same number when rounded to the nearest whole number?

3.865   3.813   4.469   4.023

Step 1. Round each of the numbers to the nearest tenth. The rounding number is in the hundredths place.

number	nearest tenth
3.865	3.9
3.813	3.8
4.469	4.5
4.023	4.0

Step 2. Round each of the numbers to the nearest whole number. The rounding number is in the tenths place.

number	nearest whole number
3.865	4
3.813	4
4.469	4
4.023	4

Step 3. Compare. 4.0 = 4

To the nearest tenth, 4.023 rounds to 4.0; to the nearest whole number, 4.023 also rounds to 4.

Read the question. Circle the answer.

1   How many numbers in the box will be 220,000 when rounded to the nearest ten thousand?

228,421	218,100	225,001	215,013

A 1   C 3

B 2   D 4

1   **B** The 4 numbers, rounded to the nearest ten thousand, are: 230,000; 220,000; 230,000; and 220,000. The second and fourth numbers round to 220,000.

Practice

Read the question. Circle the answer.

Isaac earns $1654.90 per month. The table shows the state and federal deductions that are subtracted from his monthly paycheck. Study the table. Then do number 1.

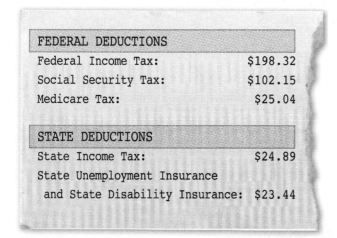

FEDERAL DEDUCTIONS	
Federal Income Tax:	$198.32
Social Security Tax:	$102.15
Medicare Tax:	$25.04

STATE DEDUCTIONS	
State Income Tax:	$24.89
State Unemployment Insurance and State Disability Insurance:	$23.44

1 After all federal and state deductions are taken out, Isaac's net monthly income is about

A $1230.00

B $1000.00

C $1500.00

D $1330.00

2 Which of these numbers when rounded to the nearest tenth is the same number when rounded to the nearest whole number?

F 5.985

G 5.799

H 6.158

J 5.813

3 Which of these numbers, when rounded to the nearest tenth, is the same number as when rounded to the nearest whole number?

A 1.973

B 1.789

C 1.652

D 2.079

Check your answers on page 123.

Lesson 40 Estimation

There are many ways you use estimation every day. You use estimation when thinking about how much you can spend at the grocery store, how much gas you can buy, how long it will take you to finish a project, and so on. When you are asked to estimate an answer, you will find an approximate answer rather than an exact answer.

Example **Marcia works as a landscape designer. The diagram shows her plan for a new client's backyard. If a 1-pound bag of fertilizer covers an area of 225 square feet, about how many pounds of fertilizer will be used to cover the back lawn?**

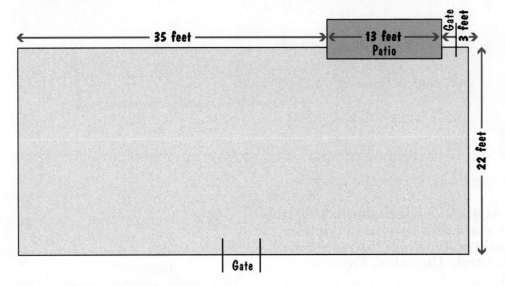

Step 1. Figure the approximate length and width of the backyard.
  Length = 35 + 13 + 3 = 51 feet, which rounds to 50.
  Width = 22 feet, which rounds to 20.

Step 2. Figure the approximate area. $A = l \times w$.
  $50 \times 20 = 1000$ square feet.

Step 3. Figure the number of fertilizer bags needed.
Round 225 square feet to 200 square feet and divide.
  $1000 \div 200 = 5$

Marcia will need about 5 pounds of fertilizer.

Test Example

Read the question. Circle the answer.

1   Marcia's design includes 20 shrubs. The price of each shrub is $46.92. Which of these is the best estimate of the total cost of the shrubs?

A $3000   C $1000

B $2000   D $4000

1 **C** You can round $46.92 to $50.00. Then multiply by 20, the number of shrubs. $50.00 × 20 = $1000.00.

Practice

Read the question. Circle the answer.

Study this advertisement for a custom-built bookcase. Then do number 1.

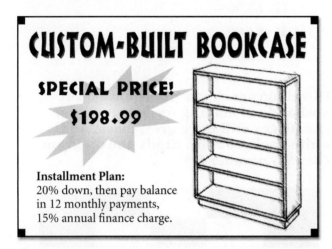

CUSTOM-BUILT BOOKCASE

SPECIAL PRICE!

$198.99

Installment Plan:
20% down, then pay balance in 12 monthly payments, 15% annual finance charge.

1 This sale price of this bookcase is 20% off the regular price. Which of these is the best estimate of the regular price of the bookcase?

A $220

B $270

C $250

D $230

2 If there are 19 dozen people in a movie theatre, about how many people are in the movie theatre?

F 150

G 100

H 250

J 200

3 The regular price for sapling maple trees at Barnes Nursery is $62.80. The trees are 25% off the regular price this week. Which of these is the best estimate of the sale price of the trees?

A $25

B $55

C $45

D $35

4 This chart shows the number of new voters who registered over the last seven weeks. Which of these is the best estimate of the average number of new voters that registered?

New Voters

Week	How Many
1	209
2	95
3	163
4	164
5	84
6	135
7	152

F 150

G 140

H 170

J 120

TABE Strategy

The word *about* signals that the answer should be an estimate.

Check your answers on page 123.

1 There is an average of 20 students per class in the Smith Middle School. There are 30 classes in the school. How many students attend Smith Middle School?

A 60

B 600

C 6000

D 6060

2 How many numbers in the box will be rounded to 160,000 when rounded to the nearest ten thousand?

| 154,523 | 158,047 | 153,979 | 154,608 |

F 1

G 2

H 3

J 4

3 Shares of stock in a company were selling for $41.25 per share. The price of a share dropped 10% last week. Which of these is the best estimate of the new price for a share of stock?

A $36

B $38

C $32

D $34

4 Vic went grocery shopping with his 20%-off-everything-in-the-store coupons. He bought orange juice for $1.69, breadcrumbs for $2.29, and eggs for $1.29. Which of these is the best estimate of how much money Vic saved by using his coupons?

F $1.00

G $3.00

H $4.00

J $2.00

This diagram shows plans for a quilt Roshanda is making for her daughter. The pieces will have grey, black, and white backgrounds. Study the diagram. Then do number 5.

5 Which of these is the best estimate of the fraction of the quilt that is covered by black pieces?

A between $\frac{1}{4}$ and $\frac{1}{3}$

B between $\frac{1}{3}$ and $\frac{1}{2}$

C between $\frac{1}{2}$ and $\frac{2}{3}$

D between $\frac{2}{3}$ and $\frac{3}{4}$

6 Helen can run a half-mile in 4 minutes. She can run 2 miles in about how many minutes?

F 5 minutes

G 16 minutes

H 8 minutes

J 10 minutes

7 Steve reads that a local TV shop is marking down all DVD players by 18% from the regular price. If a DVD player usually sells for $89.95, about how much can Steve save by buying the DVD player on sale?

A $10.00

B $30.00

C $18.00

D $25.00

8 Which of these numbers, when rounded to the nearest tenth, is the same number when rounded to the nearest whole number?

F 4.767

G 4.902

H 4.951

J 3.069

9 Gretchen earns $1858.46 per month. After deductions of $201.36, $109.32, $27.54, $22.11, and $34.17, her monthly income is about

A $1000

B $1400

C $1600

D $1500

10 A 60-pound bag of concrete mix will cover 10 square feet. About how many bags will be needed to cover an area of 147 square feet?

F 14

G 15

H 16

J 17

11 The regular price of bicycles at Main Street Bike Shop is $159.95. This week, the bicycles are on sale for 25% off the regular price. Which of these is the best estimate of the sale price of the bicycles?

A $135

B $130

C $120

D $125

Check your answers on page 123.

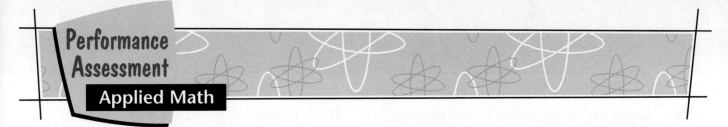

The Applied Math Assessment is identical to the real TABE in format and length. It will give you an idea of what the real test is like. Allow yourself 50 minutes to complete this assessment. Check your answers on pages 123–124.

Sample A

What number is missing from this number sequence?
3, ____, 7, 9, 11

A 2

B 4

C 5

D 6

---

1 If you start with 6, then multiply that number by 3, and then keep multiplying the number you get each time by 2, you will <u>never</u> get the number

A 144

B 72

C 288

D 96

2 Which of these is <u>not</u> enough money to buy a drink that costs $1.02?

F 3 quarters, 2 dimes, 3 nickels, 4 pennies

G 2 quarters, 3 dimes, 4 nickels, 3 pennies

H 2 quarters, 3 dimes, 3 nickels, 6 pennies

J 4 quarters, 3 dimes, 3 nickels, 2 pennies

3 Which of these is another way to show 403?

A $(4 \times 100) + (3 \times 10)$

B four hundred three

C $40 + 3$

D 4 hundreds 3 tens

4 In which of these equations is r equal to 20?

F $r - 5 = 25$

G $r + 10 = 20$

H $r - 20 = 40$

J $r + 5 = 25$

5 The graph shows the amount of money taken in at two major league baseball games in 1 night. Which of these statements is true?

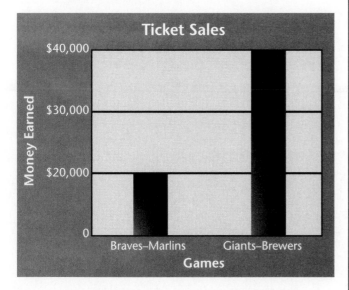

Ticket Sales

Money Earned: $40,000, $30,000, $20,000, 0

Games: Braves–Marlins, Giants–Brewers

A The Giants – Brewers game took in half as much money was made at as the Braves – Marlins game.

B The Braves – Marlins game took in $15,000 more fans than the Giants – Brewers game.

C The Giants – Brewers game took in twice as much money as the Braves – Marlins game.

D The Braves – Marlins game took in one-third less than the Giants – Brewers game.

6 A school gym has 20 rows of seating. What information is needed to find the maximum number of students who can sit in the gym?

F the number of students attending the school

G the number of students in each grade

H the number of students each row can seat

J the number of windows in the gym

7 The price of a TV is $350. If a 6% sales tax is added to this price, what is the total cost of the TV?

A $21.00

B $371.00

C $329.00

D $325.00

This chart shows the maximum growing heights of certain flowers. Study the chart. Then do number 8.

Flower Heights

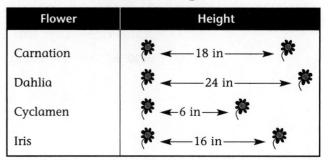

Flower	Height
Carnation	←—18 in—→
Dahlia	←——24 in——→
Cyclamen	←6 in→
Iris	←—16 in—→

Note: Heights are approximate.

8 What is the maximum height of the tallest flower?

F 18 inches

G 20 inches

H 24 inches

J 16 inches

Andy earns $1995.75 per month. This table shows the federal and state deductions that are subtracted from Andy's monthly paycheck. Study the table. Then do numbers 9 through 12.

FEDERAL DEDUCTIONS	
Federal Income Tax:	$235.04
Social Security Tax:	$117.52
Medicare Tax:	$29.38

STATE DEDUCTIONS	
State Income Tax:	$37.29
State Unemployment Insurance and State Disability Insurance:	$23.73

9 What is the total amount of federal deductions from each paycheck?

A $381.94

B $367.76

C $385.64

D $377.14

10 Andy pays 1% of his monthly income in extra health coverage. To compute this amount, he must multiply $1995.75 by

F 0.01

G 1.0

H 0.001

J 0.1

11 In which equation is n the total amount of state income tax that will be deducted from Andy's paycheck this year?

A $\dfrac{\$37.29}{12} = n$

B $\dfrac{\$1995.75}{n} = 12$

C $(n)(\$37.29) = 12$

D $(12)(\$37.29) = n$

12 After all federal and state deductions are taken out, Andy's net monthly income is about

F $1400

G $1800

H $1600

J $1300

Pam ordered a cedar chest for storing her clothes. This diagram shows the dimensions of the chest. Study the diagram. Then do numbers 13 through 16.

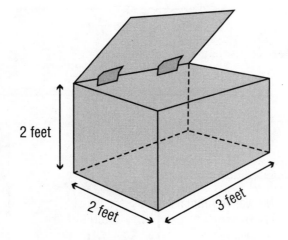

13 A 2-inch line in the diagram represents a 3-foot edge of the chest. What scale was used to draw the diagram?

A 1 inch = 1 foot

B 1 inch = $1\frac{1}{2}$ feet

C 1 inch = 2 feet

D 1 inch = $\frac{1}{2}$ foot

14 Pam decided to order a larger cedar chest with the same proportions as the cedar chest shown in the diagram. The height of the larger cedar chest will be 36 inches. What will be the length and width of the larger cedar chest?

F 54 inches × 36 inches

G 54 inches × 30 inches

H 48 inches × 36 inches

J 48 inches × 30 inches

15 Pam bought 3 sheets of special paneling to protect the inside of the chest. Each sheet costs $12.95. The sales tax is 6%. What is the total cost of the paneling? (Round to the nearest cent.)

A $41.89

B $40.78

C $42.03

D $41.18

16 How many square feet of paneling will be needed to cover the inside of the chest, including the lid?

F 16 ft^2

G 48 ft^2

H 32 ft^2

J 24 ft^2

This diagram shows the plans for a new visitor's center at the wildlife park. Study the diagram. Then do numbers 17 through 21.

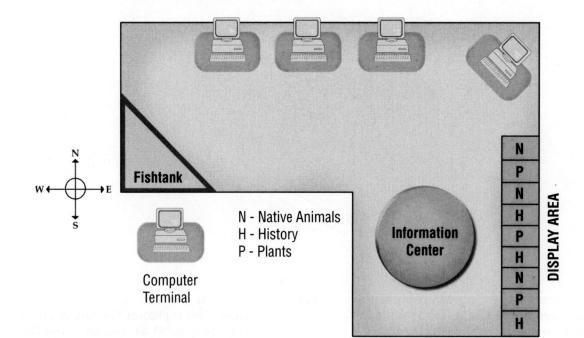

N - Native Animals
H - History
P - Plants

Computer Terminal

Information Center

DISPLAY AREA

N P N H P H N P H

17 Each computer takes an average of 7 minutes to install. About how long did it take to install all the computers?

A $\frac{1}{2}$ hour

B 1 hour

C $1\frac{1}{2}$ hours

D 2 hours

18 There will be information windows spread around the Information Center. If the windows are at 3-foot intervals, what measurement would be most convenient to determine the number of information windows needed?

F the radius

G the area

H the circumference

J the diameter

19 The workers spent $\frac{1}{2}$ of their time installing carpeting, $\frac{1}{4}$ of their time painting, $\frac{1}{3}$ of their time finishing the roof, and $\frac{1}{9}$ of their time cleaning up. The workers spent the greatest amount of time

A cleaning up

B installing carpeting

C finishing the roof

D painting

20 What kind of triangle is formed by the fish tank in the southwest corner?

F equilateral

G obtuse

H scalene

J right

21 What fractional part of the display area is devoted to native animals?

A $\frac{1}{2}$

B $\frac{1}{3}$

C $\frac{1}{4}$

D $\frac{2}{3}$

22 Which number goes in the box to make the number sentence true?

$1 \times 2 \times \square = 10$

F 10

G 5

J 25

H 2

23 Which of these decimals is less than 0.916 and greater than 0.906?

A 0.910

B 0.903

C 0.921

D 0.905

24 The table shows "Input" numbers that have been changed to "Output" numbers by applying a specific rule. What number is missing from the table?

Rule: Multiply by 2, then subtract 5.

Input	Output
6	7
8	11
11	?
15	25

F 19

G 15

H 13

J 17

25 Which of these figures is **not** a quadrilateral?

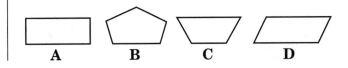

A   B   C   D

Go On ▶

This map shows the trails for Harriman Park. Study the map. Then do numbers 26 through 29.

Harriman Park

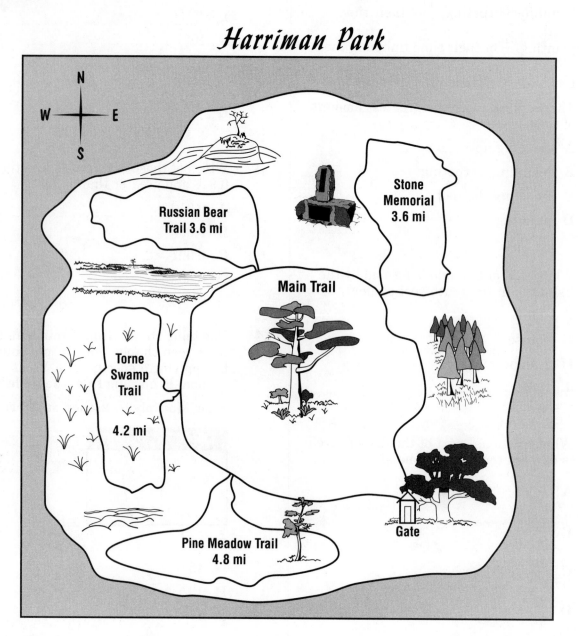

26 The distance around Stone Memorial is what fraction of the distance around Pine Meadow?

F $\frac{3}{4}$

G $\frac{1}{2}$

H $\frac{2}{3}$

J $\frac{1}{3}$

27 What is the distance in kilometers around Torne Swamp?

(1 kilometer = 0.62 miles)

A 2.49 km

B 6.77 km

C 5.95 km

D 1.53 km

28 Which of these is another way to write the distance around the Pine Meadow Trail?

F $4\frac{1}{2}$ miles

G $4\frac{8}{10}$ miles

H four and eight-hundredths miles

J 4 and two-fifths miles

29 It takes about 10 minutes to hike $\frac{1}{4}$ mile. About how long will it take to hike the Russian Bear Trail?

A 2 hours 10 minutes

B 2 hours 40 minutes

C 1 hour 20 minutes

D 2 hours 25 minutes

30 Which of these numbered triangles is similar to triangle ABC?

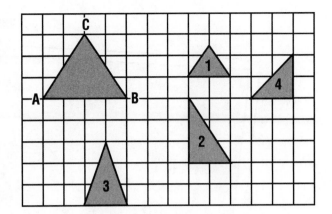

F triangle 1

G triangle 2

H triangle 3

J triangle 4

31 How many numbers in the box will be 130,000 when rounded to the nearest thousand?

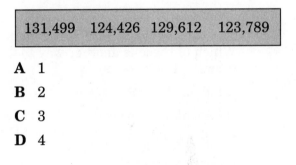

| 131,499 | 124,426 | 129,612 | 123,789 |

A 1

B 2

C 3

D 4

32 Which of these numbers when rounded to the nearest tenth is the same number when rounded to the nearest whole number?

F 8.923

G 8.799

H 9.095

J 8.973

Mr. James plans to put a gravel walkway around his property. This diagram shows the dimensions of the James' property. Study the diagram. Then do numbers 34 through 36.

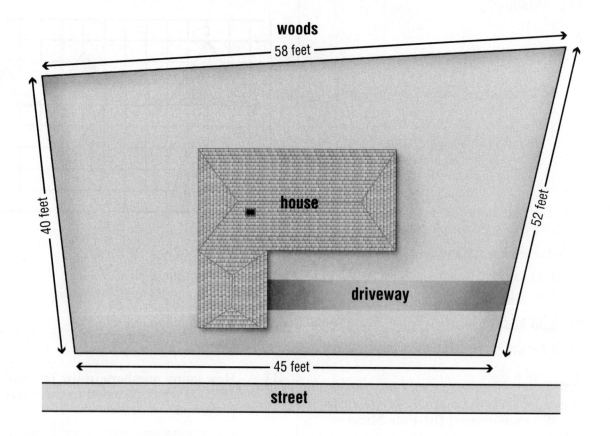

woods

58 feet

40 feet

house

52 feet

driveway

45 feet

street

33 The walkways will be 3 feet wide. Which of these is another way to describe the walkway?

   A about 50 inches wide

   B about 1 meter wide

   C about 2 yards wide

   D about 2 meters wide

34 What is the perimeter of the James' property?

   F 195 feet

   G 215 feet

   H 165 feet

   J 235 feet

35 There will be 6 birdfeeders scattered around the backyard. Every 2 birdfeeders will require a 50-pound bag of birdseed. If each bag of birdseed costs $8.75, how much will the birdseed cost?

   A $28.25

   B $35.00

   C $17.50

   D $26.25

36 There will also be a sidewalk placed between the property and the street. If the sidewalk is divided into 5-foot sections, how many sections will there be?

   F 10

   G 7

   H 9

   J 8

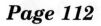

Go On

This circle graph shows the expenses of a company. Study the graph. Then do numbers 37 through 40.

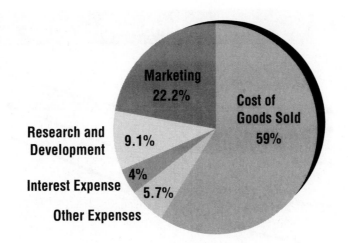

37 According to the graph, for every $100,000 of income, how much is spent on interest expense?

A $400

B $40,000

C $4000

D $400,000

38 The company recorded these expenses for one week. Which of these equations shows a way the company can use these expenses and the information in the graph to estimate their interest expense (E) for a year?

F E = (total expenses for one week) × 52 − 0.04

G E = (total expenses for one week) × 52 ÷ 0.04

H E = (total expenses for one week) × 52 × 0.04

J E = (total expenses for one week) × 12 ÷ 0.04

39 According to the graph, if the company totals its marketing, interest expense, and research and development expenses, what percent of the total expenses does this represent?

A 35.3%

B 36.3%

C 34.3%

D 37.3%

40 Last month, the cost of goods was $70,000. This month the company has reduced expenses in this area by 30%. How much did the company spend this month for the cost of goods sold?

F $59,000

G $40,000

H $49,000

J $91,000

Page 113

Go On ▶

This graph shows monthly normal temperatures from January through May for selected cities. Study the graph. Then do numbers 41 through 44.

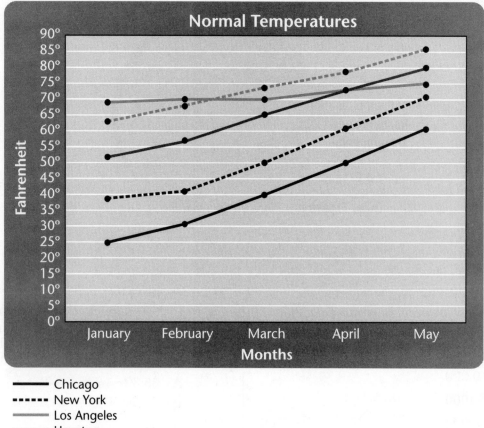

Normal Temperatures

Legend:
— Chicago
----- New York
— Los Angeles
----- Houston
— Atlanta

41 According to the graph, which city can expect the greatest increase in temperature from April to May?

A Los Angeles

B Chicago

C Atlanta

D Houston

42 Which two cities have average temperatures below 65° in four of the five months?

F New York and Chicago

G Chicago and Los Angeles

H New York and Atlanta

J Houston and Chicago

43 In May, the average temperatures from least to greatest are in

A Chicago, New York, Los Angeles, Houston, Atlanta

B New York, Chicago, Los Angeles, Atlanta, Houston

C Houston, Atlanta, Los Angeles, New York, Chicago

D Chicago, New York, Los Angeles, Atlanta, Houston

44 Which of these is the best estimate of the average temperature for all 5 cities in March?

F 55°   **H** 60°

G 50°   **J** 70°

Page 114

Go On ▶

The Smith family is going on their family vacation. They are using a road map that uses a scale of 1 inch = 30 miles. Using this information, do numbers 45 through 49.

45 What fraction of an inch equals 15 miles?

A $\dfrac{1}{8}$

B $\dfrac{1}{4}$

C $\dfrac{1}{3}$

D $\dfrac{1}{2}$

46 If the Smiths drive 120 miles, how many inches will this be on the map?

F 3 inches

G 2 inches

H 4 inches

J 5 inches

47 Gasoline costs $1.89 per gallon. How much will 10 gallons of gasoline cost?

A $189.00

B $18.90

C $1890.00

D $1.89

48 The Smith family needs to drive 300 miles. They have already driven $\dfrac{1}{3}$ the distance. If they drive the remaining distance in 4 hours, what is their average speed?

F 50 miles per hour

G 60 miles per hour

H 30 miles per hour

J 40 miles per hour

49 The scale of the map is changed to 1 inch = 40 miles. Using an actual distance of 240 miles, how would the number of inches on the map be changed?

A It would decrease by 2 inches.

B It would increase by 3 inches.

C It would increase by 2 inches.

D It would decrease by 4 inches.

50 If the pattern continues, what figure will come next?

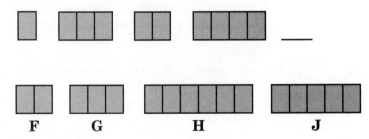

Lesson 1 Practice (page 9)

1. B sixty-three thousand seventy two and four tenths is the same as 63,072.4.

2. J seventy-five thousand fifty-eight and six tenths is the same as 75,058.6.

3. C eighty-nine thousand forty-eight and three tenths is the same as 89,048.3.

4. F sixty-four thousand one hundred three and seven tenths.

Lesson 2 Practice (page 11)

1. C four hundred eight thousand two hundred fifty-six is the same as 408,256.

2. F Three hundred seven is the same as 307.

3. D 2797 is the same as two thousand seven hundred ninety-seven.

4. G $(8 \times 100) = 800$; $(4 \times 10) = 40$. $800 + 40 = 840$.

5. A Fifty thousand ninety-three is the same as 50,093.

6. F Four hundred seven is the same as 407.

Lesson 3 Practice (page 13)

1. D Add these numbers together.

$$\begin{array}{r} 40,000,000 \\ 1,000,000 \\ +\underline{\qquad 9} \\ 41,000,009 \end{array}$$

2. F $30,000 + 5,000 + 60 + 9 = 35,069$

3. C Add the numbers together.

$$\begin{array}{r} 90,000,000 \\ 2,000,000 \\ 900,000 \\ 50,000 \\ 5,000 \\ +\underline{\qquad 800} \\ 92,955,800 \end{array}$$

4. G Add the numbers together.

$$\begin{array}{r} 800,000 \\ 6,000 \\ 500 \\ 90 \\ +\underline{\qquad 3} \\ 806,593 \end{array}$$

5. B
$$\begin{array}{rl} 1 \times 10,000,000 = & 10,000,000 \\ 2 \times 1,000,000 = & 2,000,000 \\ 4 \times 100,000 = & 400,000 \\ 1 \times 10,000 = & 10,000 \\ 9 \times 1,000 = & 9,000 \\ 2 \times 100 = & 200 \\ 9 \times 10 = & 90 \\ 3 \times 1 = \qquad + & \underline{\qquad 3} \\ & 12,419,293 \end{array}$$

6. H Add the numbers together.

Lesson 4 Practice (page 15)

1. C The hundredths place is greater than 2, and the thousandths place is less than 8.

2. F $\frac{7}{8}$, $\frac{3}{5}$, and $\frac{3}{4}$ have lower top numbers than bottom numbers.

3. D First, look at the tenths. Then look at hundredths places.

Lesson 5 Practice (page 17)

1. A Find the east section. There are 6 equal sections. Of the 6 sections, 2 are luxury seating. $\frac{2}{6}$ can be rewritten as $\frac{1}{3}$.

2. H Netz Place is 0.6 miles in length and Willis Avenue has a length of 2.4 miles. The top and bottom numbers of $\frac{0.6}{2.4}$ may be divided by 0.6, which results in the fraction $\frac{1}{4}$.

Lesson 6 Practice (page 19)

1. B Each of the points on the number line is 0.01 apart.

2. J Each of the points on the number line is 0.01 apart.

3. A Each of the points on the number line is 0.02 apart.

4. F Each of the points on the number line is 0.04 apart.

5. A Each of the points on the number line is .02 more than the point to its left. One point to the left of 0.49 is 0.47.

6. J There are two segments on the number line between 0.55 and 0.57. The difference between these numbers is 0.02 This tells you that each segment of the number line represents 0.01 (0.02 ÷ 2 = 0.01). The box is four segments up the number line from 0.57. $0.57 + 4(0.01) = 0.57 + 0.04 = 0.61$.

7. B Wednesday is the only day in the chart with a snowfall amount of 0.06 inches.

8. J Each point on the number line is .01 apart. The box is at 0.10.

TABE Review: Numeration (pages 20–21)

1. C 360,395 is the same as three hundred sixty thousand three hundred ninety-five. [Recognizing Numbers]

2. J The odometer may be read as thirty-five thousand twenty-seven and eight tenths. [Word Names]

3. B 40% is written as $\frac{40}{100}$, which may be reduced to $\frac{2}{5}$.

[Fractional Part]

4. H The height may be written as one thousand eight hundred fifteen feet. [Word Names]

5. D 14 of the 24 sections ($\frac{14}{24}$) will be planted with flowers, which may be reduced to $\frac{7}{12}$.

[Fractional Part]

6. F 56,889 is the same as 50,000 + 6,000 + 800 + 80 + 9. [Expanded Notation]

7. A 3508 is written as three thousand five hundred eight. [Recognizing Numbers]

8. J $\frac{5}{4}$ and $\frac{3}{2}$ are greater than 1. [Comparison]

9. C If 5 chips take up an inch, 3 chips would take up $\frac{3}{5}$ inch of space. [Fractional Part]

10. G Each of the points on the number line increases by 0.02. [Number Line]

11. B 13,764,000 is the same as 10,000,000 + 3,000,000 + 700,000 + 60,000 + 4,000. [Expanded Notation]

12. F Each point on the number line increases by 0.01. [Number Line]

13. B $\frac{4}{12}$ is reduced to $\frac{1}{3}$. [Fractional Part]

14. J 0.519 is the only decimal between 0.503 and 0.561 [Number Line]

Lesson 7 Practice (page 23)

1. D 5.5 is the same as $5\frac{1}{2}$.

2. G 0.35 is the same as $\frac{35}{100}$. Reduced to its simplest form, it is $\frac{7}{20}$.

3. A The decimal 0.70 is less than 0.75, 0.78, and 0.79.

4. G If 0.25 of all customers are children, then that is the same as $\frac{25}{100}$, or $\frac{1}{4}$.

5. C When all fractions are simplified and compared, the same number of tutors will be assigned to Reading and Study Skills.

6. F $\frac{3}{4}$ is the same as $\frac{75}{100}$, which is the decimal 0.75.

Lesson 8 Practice (page 25)

1. B Setting up the scale as a fraction $\frac{2}{6}$, we see the ratio is 1 inch = 3 feet when we reduce the fraction.

2. J The ratio of the length of Stan's patio to Sarah's is 22:11 or 2. The width of Sarah's patio is 10 feet. If this ratio is applied, the width of Stan's patio will be 20 feet.

Lesson 9 Practice (page 27)

1. A Multiply $95.99 × 0.07 = $6.72 sales tax on each CD player. If each CD player will cost $102.71 ($95.99 + $6.72), then 2 CD players will be $205.42 ($102.71 × 2).

2. H 5% is written as 0.05 in decimal form.

3. B 20% of $30 is $6 (30 × 0.20), so the special rate is $24 ($30 − $6). This rate is multiplied by 103 hours to find the cost of $2472 for snow removal.

4. F 6% of $50 is $3 (50 × 0.06 = $3). This is added to 50 for the full cost of $53.

5. D 20% of $50 is $10 ($50 × 0.20).

TABE Review: Number Theory (pages 28–29)

1. B 2.6 is the same as $2\frac{6}{10}$. This may be reduced to $2\frac{3}{5}$. [Equivalent Form]

2. F 10% is the same as 0.10. [Percent]

3. C Divide 600 by 2, so the scale is 1 inch = 300 miles. [Ratio and Proportion]

4. G The distance from north to south is $\frac{2}{3}$ of the distance from east to west $\left(\frac{2000}{3000}\right)$. On the smaller section, the distance from east to west will be 1500 miles. [Ratio and Proportion]

5. D 0.25 is the same as $\frac{25}{100}$. This may be reduced to $\frac{1}{4}$.

[Equivalent Form]

6. H There are 7 people living on each square mile of land (14 ÷ 2). To find the number of people living on 10 square miles of land multiply 10 × 7 = 70. [Ratio and Proportion]

7. A 0.30 is the same as $\frac{30}{100}$. This may be reduced to $\frac{6}{20}$. [Equivalent Form]

8. H $\frac{3}{12} = \frac{1}{4}$, which is the same as 1 inch = 4 feet.

[Ratio and Proportion]

9. B Multiply 5.60 × 0.07, which is 0.39 tax on each dozen. The total cost of a dozen is $5.99 ($5.60 + 0.39). The cost of 2 dozen is $11.98 ($5.99 × 2). [Percent]

10. H Multiply 1600 × 0.20 to find how much less they'll weigh in a bad year. They will weigh 1280 pounds (1600 − 320). Multiply this weight by 5 to find the answer of 6400 pounds. [Percent]

11. A 75% is the same as $\frac{75}{100}$. This may be reduced to $\frac{3}{4}$.

[Percent]

12. G 60 ÷ 80 = 0.75. This is the same as 75%. If they won 75%, they lost 25% of their games (100 − 75). [Percent]

13. C 20% off a full price of $5 would result in a reduced price of $4. [Percent]

14. F If there is an extra 10% off for 10 or more books, this will result in a savings of $0.40 per book. You will save $4.00 (0.40 × 10). [Percent]

Lesson 10 Practice (page 31)

1. B In 1991, the lines for men's and women's sports participation are farthest apart.

2. J During this time period, there was an increase of about 10,000 women from the last period.

3. C The bar showing housing is the highest for this age group.

4. F The bar for food is about half as high as the bar for housing for this age group.

Lesson 11 Practice (page 33)

1. D When the numbers of barrels of oil are arranged from least to greatest, 500 million is the number in the middle.

Lesson 12 Practice (page 35)

1. B Bulgur wheat has 26.5 grams of fiber.

2. J Clarksdale has the most restaurants.

3. C Find the average by adding 68 + 97 + 35 + 80 + 75 = 355, divide by 5 = 71. 71 rounds down to 70.

4. H Nashville scored 70 points.

5. D Ottawa has scored 80 points and Minnesota has scored 90 points. Together they have scored 170 points (90 + 80).

6. J Minnesota has scored 90 points and Nashville has scored 70 points (90 − 70 = 20).

Lesson 13 Practice (page 37)

1. C The number of seats in each row is needed to find the number of people the arena can seat.

2. F The total number of tickets sold is needed to find out how many were sold per performance.

3. A The first step in finding the average height is to add the height of the three buildings. You need the height of the Sears Tower.

4. H The cost of the buns is needed.

5. C The number of Saturn's known moons is needed to find the total number of moons for the three planets.

6. G The number of refugees who entered Canada is needed to find the total number of refugees for both the United States and Canada.

7. B The number of Ted's friends is needed to solve this problem.

8. G The length of the phone call is needed to find the cost of the call.

TABE Review: Data Interpretation (pages 38–39)

1. A If you know how long it took him to read each book, you can find the time it took him to read 25 books [Pre-Solution]

2. H 60 is the middle, or median, number. [Probability and Statistics]

3. A Travel showed the greatest increase from year 4 to year 5. [Graphs]

4. H $27,500 + $35,000 + $40,000 + $45,000 = $147,500, or about $150,000. [Graphs]

5. G Find year 4 and list the expenses from least to greatest. [Graphs]

6. B Less is spent on travel in the fourth year than the second year. [Graphs]

7. C The number of pounds of chicken Wayne bought is needed. [Pre-Solution]

8. F Round each number to the nearest ten and add: $290 + $220 + $330 + $200 + $270 + $250 + $150 = $1710 ÷ 7 = 244.3, which is rounded to $240. [Charts]

9. B $400 × 0.04 = $16 tax, which is added to $400. $400 + $16 = $416 [Charts]

10. G The number of seats in each row is needed to determine the number of people the school theater can seat. [Pre-Solution]

11. A Mining products make up the smallest percentage of imports. [Charts]

12. G 30% + 27% + 7% = 64% [Charts]

Lesson 14 Practice (page 41)

1. C 60 seconds is 3 times as long as 20 seconds. Multiply 6 × 3 for the answer of 18 envelopes.

2. F 2 × 3 = 6, 6 × 3 = 18, 18 × 3 = 54, 54 × 3 = 162. You will never get the number 52.

3. D Each input number is divided by 5. 40 ÷ 5 = 8.

4. H Sound travels 350 meters per second (700 ÷ 2). In 10 seconds, it would travel 3500 meters (350 × 10).

5. A 6 × 4 − 2 = 22

6. G The pattern is + 400 and then + 500. If it increases by 600 between 1980 and 2000, there will be 1800 (1200 + 600) billion miles traveled.

Lesson 15 Practice (page 43)

1. D 4 × 5 × 3 = 60

2. H 5 × 2 × 5 = 50

3. D Set up a proportion. $\frac{2}{5} = \frac{\square}{15}$. Tran will need 6 parts lemon juice.

4. J 4 × 2 × 2 = 16

5. B 5 × 2 = 10; 10 × 2 = 20. If you repeat this 2 more times you will get 80 and 320. You will never get 30.

6. F 2 × 15 × 3 = 90

7. D 100 + 119 + 114 = 333; 442 − 333 = 109.

8. H $\frac{5}{6}$, $\frac{3}{4}$, and $\frac{2}{3}$ are less than 1.

1. **B** If 35 pages are read in 1 hour, the number sentence $35 \times 3 = \square$ can be used to find the number of pages read in 3 hours.

2. **F** If Ed had 13 pairs of socks and threw out 5 pairs, the number sentence $13 - 5 = \square$ can be used.

3. **C** If there were 50 bison in 1950 and 5 times that in 2001, use the number sentence $50 \times 5 = \square$ to find the number of bison in 2001.

4. **J** The number sentence $80 \div 5 = \square$ could be used to find how many pens Phyllis could give each customer.

5. **A** If Luisa ran 24 miles in 4 hours, the number sentence $24 \div 4 = \square$ shows the average number of miles she ran each hour.

6. **F** Paul needs to use the number sentence $6 \times 2 = \square$ to find how many sausages he will need, which is 12.

7. **A** Jordanna can use the number sentence $20 \times 3 = \square$ to find out the number of cookies she needs to bake.

8. **G** The number sentence $\$20 + \$9 = \square$ can be used to show that Chuck saved $29.

1. **D** If Clark can buy 4 pencils for $1.00, he can buy 5 times as many for $5.00. $4 \times 5 = 20$.

2. **F** If you substitute 20 for b, $20 + 5 = 25$.

3. **B** There are 12 months in a year, and $27.44 is taken from Barbara's pay check each month. $(12)(\$27.44)$ or $12 \times \$27.44$ equals the amount Barbara will pay in Medicare tax for the year.

4. **H** If you multiply the number of fans per game (8,184) $\times$ 82, you will find the total number of fans for the season. 30% is equal to 0.30. The total number of fans multiplied by 0.30 will give you an estimate of the number of hot dogs sold.

5. **A** You know there are 60 minutes in an hour. There are five 12-minute periods in an hour ($60 \div 12 = 5$). By multiplying 3×5, you find the number of miles Renee can run in an hour.

6. **G** Dividing $4011 by $3.00 gives the number of visitors for the week. Since there are 7 days in a week, dividing this result by 7 gives the average number of visitors to the lighthouse each day.

7. **B** $38 - 6 = 32$

1. **C** By changing $\frac{1}{2}$ to $\frac{2}{4}$ and adding all the fractions, you have a total of $1\frac{1}{4}$ cups.

2. **F** $\frac{7}{8} + \frac{3}{4} + \frac{1}{4} = \frac{7}{8} + \frac{6}{8} + \frac{2}{8} = \frac{15}{8} = 1\frac{7}{8}$. Kathy gives her dogs $1\frac{7}{8}$ cups of food daily.

3. **B** $\frac{5}{12} + \frac{2}{6} + \frac{4}{12} = \frac{5}{12} + \frac{4}{12} + \frac{4}{12} = \frac{13}{12} = 1\frac{1}{12}$ cups of seeds needed.

4. **J** $\frac{2}{3} + \frac{2}{6} + \frac{5}{6} = \frac{4}{6} + \frac{2}{6} + \frac{5}{6} = \frac{11}{6} = 1\frac{5}{6}$ cans of stain used.

5. **A** The second car was traveling at 40 miles per hour. $60 - 20 = 40$.

1. **B** At 3 cookies per dollar, y is the greatest number of cookies Sasha can buy with $5.00 dollars. [Equations]

2. **H** When you bring + 15 to the other side of the equal sign, you find $25 - 15 = 10$. [Equations]

3. **A** First change $\frac{1}{2}$ to $\frac{2}{4}$. Then add $\frac{1}{4} + \frac{2}{4} + \frac{3}{4} = \frac{6}{4}$ or $1\frac{1}{2}$. [Applied Algebra]

4. **F** First divide the $8.00 Billy had to spend by the cost of 3 donuts ($2.00). $8 \div 2 = 4$. Now the equation $3 \times 4 = n$ may be used to find n, the number of donuts Billy bought. [Equations]

5. **A** She plays tennis 2 hours a day, 3 days a week. [Equations]

6. **J** $n = 35 - 20$; $n = 15$ [Number Sentences]

7. **B** The equation shows how many grapefruits Nina can buy for $1.00 (4), times the number of dollars she has (3), which equals the number of grapefruits she can buy for $3.00. Nina has $3.00 to spend, not $4.00 (option A). The amount of money Nina has altogether is not part of the problem or the equation (option C). The amount of money Nina has to spend on grapefruits is only <u>part</u> of the question (option D). [Equations]

8. **F** Write the information as a proportion. The recipe calls for 10 ounces of chicken for 6 people, or $\frac{10}{6}$. You need to find out how many ounces of chicken feed 12 people, or $\frac{n}{12}$. $\frac{n}{12} = \frac{10}{6}$, or $n = \frac{10}{6} \times 12$. [Equations]

9. **C** $4 \times 2 \times \square = 40$. $\square = 40 \div 8 = 5$. [Missing Element]

10. **J** $7 \times 2 = \underline{14}$. $14 \times 2 = \underline{28}$. $28 \times 2 = \underline{56}$. $56 \times 2 = \underline{112}$. Vick will <u>never</u> get 49. [Functions and Patterns]

11. **C** The rule is $\frac{1}{2} \times$ the "Input" number = the "Output" number. The missing "Output" number is $\frac{1}{2} \times 50 = 25$. [Functions and Pattern]

12. **G** Use $5 + 3 + \square = 10$. This becomes $8 + \square = 10$. Then $10 - 8 = 2$ red pens. [Applied Algebra]

13. **D** 89×6 will tell how far the airplane could fly in 6 hours. [Number Sentences]

14. H Use 5×20 to show the number of seeds. Because 70% is equal to 0.70, the equation becomes $(5 \times 20) \times 0.70$ to find the number of plants expected. [Applied Algebra]

Lesson 19 Practice (page 53)

1. B 2 quarters = $0.50, + 2 dimes = $0.20, and + 15 pennies = $0.15. $0.50 + $0.20 + $0.15 = $0.85 total.

2. J $0.15 \times 100 = $15.00

3. A ($3 \times 1 = $3.00) + ($10 \times 2 = $20.00) + ($0.25 \times 2 = $0.50) + ($0.10 \times 5 = $0.50) + ($0.01 \times 6 = $0.06) = $24.06

4. H $15.35 \times 10 = $153.50

5. B (3 \times $0.05 + (1 \times $0.25) = $0.15 + $0.25 = $0.40

6. F 3($0.25) + 4($0.10) + 3($0.05) = $0.75 + $0.40 + $0.15 = $1.30

Lesson 20 Practice (page 55)

1. A Add 6:10 + 6:20 = 12:30, or $12\frac{1}{2}$ hours.

2. G Des Moines is in the Central Time Zone, so it is 1 hour earlier in Des Moines than it is in Columbus, which is in the Eastern Time Zone.

Lesson 21 Practice (page 57)

1. A Since there are 3 feet in a yard, divide $9 \div 3 = 3$ yards.

2. H Change 8 feet to yards. There are 2 yards ($2 \times 3 = 6$) and 2 feet left over.

3. D To change feet to meters, multiply $23 \times 0.3048 = 7.0104$, which is about 7 meters.

4. F To change inches to yards, divide $36 \div 12 = 3$ feet, or 1 yard.

5. D Multiply feet times inches per foot $42 \times 12 = 504$ inches wide.

6. H Multiply $484 \times 3 = 1452$ feet.

7. B Only Monday and Wednesday have fractions with a greater top number than bottom number.

Lesson 22 Practice (page 59)

1. D Add $96 + 83 + 92 + 87 = 358$ feet.

2. F If the measure from north to south is 280 miles, and the measure from east to west is 360, the perimeter is $280 + 280 + 360 + 360 = 1280$ miles.

3. B Since a soccer field is a rectangle, find the perimeter by adding $361 + 361 + 246 + 246 = 1214$ feet.

4. H Each side of a square is equal. 6 inches $\times 4 = 24$ inches.

5. D Since a triangle has 3 sides, add $12 + 13 + 20 = 45$ inches.

6. F Add $7 + 3 + 8 + 12 + 1 + 9 = 40$ yards.

Lesson 23 Practice (page 61)

1. B To find the area, multiply 8 feet $\times$ 10 feet = 80 square feet.

2. F The town measures 8 miles $\times$ 4 miles = 32 square miles. 32 square miles $\div$ 2 square mile-section = 16 sections.

3. A 96 inches = 8 feet. 32 square feet $\div$ 8 feet = 4 feet.

4. J 24 inches $\times$ 36 inches = 2 feet $\times$ 3 feet = 6 square feet

5. B 48 inches $\times$ 60 inches = 4 feet $\times$ 5 feet = 20 square feet. Option A is 60 square feet, option C is 63 square feet, and option D is 70 square feet.

6. G 48 inches $\times$ 120 inches = 4 feet $\times$ 10 feet = 40 square feet. Sandra will need 1 bag to cover 30 square feet, plus a second bag to cover the remaining 10 square feet.

7. D The size of the track is needed to determine miles per hour.

Lesson 24 Practice (page 63)

1. A 5 gallons $\times$ 3.79 liters/gallon = 18.95 liters.

2. H 18 feet $\times$ 10 feet $\times$ 6 feet = 1080 cubic feet.

3. B 40 inches $\times$ 15 inches $\times$ 12 inches = 7200 cubic inches.

4. J First multiply $2 \times 3 = 6$. Then divide 24 square feet $\div$ 6 feet = 4 feet for the length of the box.

5. C Multiply 8 feet $\times$ 12 feet $\times$ 8 feet = 768 cubic feet

6. G Multiply 7 centimeters $\times$ 7 centimeters $\times$ 19 centimeters = 931 cubic centimeters.

Lesson 25 Practice (page 65)

1. D Top and bottom = $2 \times (5 \times 3) = 30$
Front and back = $2 \times (5 \times 3) = 30$
Left and right sides = $2 \times (3 \times 3) = 18$
$30 + 30 + 18 = 78$

2. F Top and bottom = $2 \times (20 \times 5) = 200$
Front and back = $2 \times (20 \times 30) = 1200$
Left and right sides = $2 \times (30 \times 5) = 300$
$200 + 1200 + 300 = 1700$

3. B Top and bottom = $2 \times (4 \times 3) = 24$
Front and back = $2 \times (4 \times 6) = 48$
Left and right sides = $2 \times (6 \times 3) = 36$
$24 + 48 + 36 = 108$

4. J Top and bottom = $2 \times (4 \times 4) = 32$
Front and back = $2 \times (4 \times 6) = 48$
Left and right sides = $2 \times (6 \times 4) = 48$
$32 + 48 + 48 = 128$

5. C Top = $1 \times (15 \times 11) = 165$
Front and back = $2 \times (15 \times 8) = 240$
Left and right sides = $2 \times (8 \times 11) = 176$
$165 + 240 + 176 = 581$

6. H Top and bottom = $2 \times (4 \times n) = 8n$
Front and back = $2 \times (3 \times 4) = 24$
Left and right sides = $2 \times (3 \times n) = 6n$
$24 + 8n + 6n = 24 + 14n = 164$
$14n = 164 - 24 = 140$
$n = 140 \div 14 = 10$

1. D (3 × $0.25) + (4 × $0.10) + (6 × $0.05) + (5 × $0.01) = $0.75 + $0.40 + $0.30 + $0.05 = $1.50 [Money]

2. F Regroup by adding 60 minutes to 00:05, and subtracting 1 hour from 9:00. 8:65 − 7:15 = 1:50. [Time]

3. C There are 12 inches in a foot. 12 inches/foot × 6 feet = 72 inches. [Length]

4. G 54 feet × 0.3048 meters/foot = 16.4592 meters or about 16.5 meters. [Length]

5. A 12 feet × 11 feet = 132 square feet. [Area]

6. J (2 × (3 × 2)) + (2 × (3 × 4)) + (2 × (4 × 2)) = 52 square inches. [Surface Area]

7. B Cliff would receive $2.35 in change. (7 × $0.25) + (5 × $0.10) + (1 × $0.05) + (5 × $0.01) = $1.75 + $0.50 + $ 0.05 + $0.05 = $2.35. [Money]

8. G Regroup by adding 60 minutes to 00:07 and regroup by subtracting 1 hour from 11:00. 10:67 − 6:55 = 4:12. [Time]

9. A Bus 611 takes 3 hours and 20 minutes. [Time]

10. H Bus 823 leaves at 9:15 a.m. Yolanda has to leave the house 45 minutes before this. 9:15 − 0:45 = 8:30. [Time]

11. B 60 feet + 51 feet + 102 feet + 96 feet = 309 feet [Perimeter]

12. H 9 inches × 12 inches = 108 square inches. [Area]

13. A 25 gallons × 3.79 liters/gallon = 94.75 liters [Volume and Capacity]

Lesson 26 Practice (page 69)

1. D An 8-sided figure is an octagon.

2. F A parallelogram has exactly 2 sets of parallel lines.

3. B A 5-sided figure is a pentagon.

4. J A rectangle is a parallelogram. None of the other options list figures that fit the definition of a parallelogram.

5. C A rectangle has exactly two pair of parallel lines. Option A has 4 pairs of parallel lines. Options B and D have no pairs of parallel lines.

6. H A square is the only quadrilateral listed in the answer choices.

Lesson 27 Practice (page 71)

1. C The original figure was a rectangular prism, which is cut to make a rectangular prism and a cube.

2. F Earth is a sphere.

3. B The oatmeal container is a cylinder.

4. F The figure contains a cube and a rectangular prism.

5. C This figure is a rectangular pyramid.

6. H Options F, G, and J are not true statements.

Lesson 28 Practice (page 73)

1. B The pattern is to add 1 rectangle to each group.

2. F Each figure in the pattern increases by 2 parallelograms.

3. C Each figure increases by 2 more blocks than the figure before it.

4. F The next arrow will be pointing left.

Lesson 29 Practice (page 75)

1. C Figures 1 and 3 are the same size and shape. Figure 7 is a quadrilateral and 4 is a triangle. Figure 10 is much larger than 4. Figures 5 and 2 are different, irregular shapes.

2. F These figures are the same size and shape, but are facing different directions. They are still congruent.

3. A The figure contains 6 triangles that all are congruent.

Lesson 30 Practice (page 77)

1. A The sum of the angles in a triangle is 180°. Add 81° + 43° = 124°. Then subtract 180° − 124° = 56°.

2. H Add the sum of the two known angles: 36° + 70° = 106°. Then subtract 180° − 106° = 74 degrees.

3. B Add the sum of the two known angles: 32° + 59° = 91°. Then subtract 180° − 91° = 89 degrees.

4. G Add the sum of the two known angles: 21° + 76° = 97°. Then subtract 180° − 97° = 83 degrees.

Lesson 31 Practice (page 79)

1. C The sum of the angles in a triangle is 180°. Add the sum of the two known angles: 49° + 65° = 114°. Then subtract 180° − 114° = 66 degrees.

2. J This triangle has three equal sides.

3. C Triangle 5 is the only triangle in the figure with an obtuse angle.

4. H If it is equilateral, all three sides are equal, so all the angles must be equal. 60° × 3 = 180°

Lesson 32 Practice (page 81)

1. A Similar figures are the same shape but can be of different sizes.

2. J Figure D is the same shape but a different size.

3. C Both triangles FGH and triangle 3 are equilateral triangles, but they are different sizes.

4. F Similar figures are the same shape but different size.

Lesson 33 Practice (page 83)

1. C The diameter is a line that passes through the center of the circle.

2. G The radius connects the center to a point on the circle.

3. C If the pool is 48 inches across, she needs a cover with a diameter of at least 48 inches.

4. H The area shows the number of square units needed to cover a circle.

5. D Mr. Saunders will need to know the circumference.

TABE Review: Geometry (pages 84–85)

1. A Each group has one more row and column of shapes than the group before it. The next group will contain 16. [Patterns and Shapes]

2. F Congruent figures have the same shape and size. [Congruency]

3. B Similar figures are the same shape but different size. [Similarity]

4. H Two sides of this figure are not parallel. [Plane Figures]

5. C $180 - (62 + 37) = 180 - 99 = 81$ degrees. [Angles]

6. H An isosceles triangle has 2 equal sides. [Triangles]

7. C She will need to know the area of the circle. [Parts of a Circle]

8. H One of the angles is a right angle. [Triangles]

9. B This figure is a cube. [Solid Figures]

10. F The window is a hexagon. [Plane Figures]

Lesson 34 Practice (page 87)

1. D The north side of the yard measures 96 feet. $96 \div 6 = 16$ sections of fencing needed.

2. J From Miami to Jacksonville to Atlanta is 723.

3. C It is 50° at 12 a.m. and 75° at 4 p.m. $75° - 50° = 25°$.

4. J It is 55° at 6 a.m. and 70° at 12 p.m. $70° - 55° = 15°$.

Lesson 35 Practice (page 89)

1. D Since each bag is enough for 2 cakes, they will need 5 bags for 10 cakes. $5 \times \$2.99$ per bag $= \$14.95$.

2. G Divide $3.1 \div 0.62$ to find that 5 kilometers were run.

3. C Add all the expenses ($\$1086.41$) and subtract from Clark's salary ($\$1978.64$).

4. H Divide $3.7 \div 0.62 = 5.97$ km.

5. B First multiply $2 \times \$12.75 = \$25.50$. This is subtracted from $\$40.00$ to find the change of $\$14.50$.

6. F If each roll will finish every 3 of the twelve windows, 4 rolls are needed. Multiply $4 \times \$9.53$.

Lesson 36 Practice (page 91)

1. B Change $23\frac{1}{2}$ to $\frac{47}{2}$. Multiply this by 3: $\frac{47}{2} \times \frac{3}{1} = \frac{141}{2} = 70\frac{1}{2}$ pounds.

2. J First find the number of square feet by multiplying. $23\frac{1}{2} \times 15 = \frac{47}{2} \times \frac{15}{1} = \frac{705}{2}$. To find the number

of tiles needed, divide. $\frac{705}{2} \div 2\frac{1}{2} = \frac{705}{2} \div \frac{5}{2} = \frac{705}{2} \times \frac{2}{5} = \frac{1410}{10}$. Simplify to 141 tiles needed to tile the ceiling.

3. C Multiply $1\frac{1}{2} \times 2 = 3$ pounds of ground beef.

4. H Divide $\frac{1}{2} \div 2 = \frac{1}{4}$ cup of breadcrumbs.

Lesson 37 Practice (page 93)

1. A Multiply. $\$15.75 \times 3 = \$47.25$. This is multiplied by 0.06 to find the sales tax of $\$2.84$. The total cost is $\$47.25 + \$2.84 = \$50.09$.

2. H Multiply $100,000 \times 0.25 = 25,000$ people.

3. B Add $7.9\% + 5.9\% = 13.8\%$.

4. J First add $\$3.49 + \$3.49 = \$6.98$. Then multiply to find the tax amount: $\$6.98 \times 0.06 = 0.4188$. Round this to the nearest cent: 0.42. Add the tax to the total dollar amount: $0.42 + 6.98 = \$7.40$.

5. A Divide $130 \div 520 = 0.25$, or 25%.

6. H 20% is equal to $\frac{20}{100}$. This reduces to $\frac{1}{5}$.

7. B $\frac{1}{2}$ is the same as 50% ($\frac{1}{2} = \frac{50}{100}$).

TABE Review: Computation in Context (page 94–95)

1. D Multiply. $\$80 \times 0.35 = \$28$ shipping charge. This is added to the $\$80$ for a total of $\$108$. [Percents in context]

2. G Multiply $\$120 \times 0.10$ to find the $\$12$ discount. The shipping is based on $\$108 \times 0.20 = \$21.60$. Added to $\$108$, the total is $\$129.60$. [Percents in context]

3. B Divide 9 by $\frac{3}{4}$. This is done by $\frac{9}{1} \times \frac{4}{3} = \frac{36}{3} = 12$ breaks on the hike. [Fractions in context]

4. G Multiply $\frac{140}{1} \times \frac{1}{2} = 70$ decibels. [Fractions in context]

5. A Multiply $100 \times .20 = 20$ decibels. This is added to 100 decibels for a level of 120 decibels. [Decimals in context]

Lesson 38 Practice (page 97)

1. C Divide $60 \div 10 = 6$ families per square mile.

2. G $\frac{3}{10} = 0.30$, which fits between $\frac{1}{4}$ (0.25) and $\frac{1}{3}$ (0.33).

3. C Multiply $5 \times 3 = 15$ miles per week. Remove the 0 in 20 to simplify the problem. Multiply $15 \times 2 = 30$. Then put back the 0 from 20 to get 300.

4. F Divide. $13 \div 4 = 3.25$, which is about 3 inches

Lesson 39 Practice (page 99)

1. D First round the 3-digit dollar amounts to the nearest 100: $198.32 rounds to $200.00; $102.15 rounds to $100.00. Round the 2-digit dollar amounts to the nearest 10: $25.04 rounds to $25.00; $24.89 rounds to $25.00; and $23.44 rounds to $20.00. Add the rounded numbers 200 + 100 + 30 + 20 + 20 = 370. Next, round the amount Isaac earns per month: $1654.90 rounds to $1700.00 Subtract. $1700 − $370.00 = $1330.00

2. F When rounded to the nearest whole number, 5.985 is 6, and when rounded to the nearest tenth, it is the same number.

3. A When rounded to the nearest whole number, 1.973 is 2. When rounded to the nearest tenth, it is also 2.

Lesson 40 Practice (page 101)

1. C First round $198.99 to $200. $200 × 20% = $200 × 0.2 = $40. $200 + $ 40 = $240. If the sale price is about $200 with a 20% discount from full price, the full price is about $250.

2. J One dozen is 12, which may be rounded to 10. Multiply 19 × 10 = 190, which can be rounded to 200.

3. C First $62.80 can be rounded to $60.00. 25% of this amount can be found by multiplying 60 × 0.25 = 15. This is subtracted from $60.00 for an estimated amount of $45.00.

4. G Add the numbers then divided by 7. The result, 143.1, is rounded down to 140.

TABE Review: Estimation (pages 102–103)

1. B Multiply 20 × 30 = 600. [Reasonableness of Answer]

2. F Rounded to the nearest ten thousand, 158,047; is 160,000 [Rounding]

3. A Round $41.25 to $40. Next multiply $40 × 0.10 = $4 drop per share. This leaves a new price of $36 ($40 − $4). [Rounding]

4. F Round $1.69 to $2, $2.29 to $2 and $1.29 to $1. Add 2 + 2 + 1 = 5. Multiply 5 × 0.20 = 1 = $1.00. [Rounding]

5. B $\frac{4}{10}$ = 0.40, which is between $\frac{1}{3}$ (0.33) and $\frac{1}{2}$ (0.50). [Reasonableness of Answer]

6. G Because she can run a half mile in 4 minutes, and there are 4 half miles in 2 miles, multiply 4 × 4 = 16 minutes to run 2 miles [Estimation]

7. C Round 18% to 0.20 and $89.95 to $90. Multiply $90 × 0.20 = $18. [Estimation]

8. H When rounded to the nearest whole number, 4.951 is 5; and when rounded to the nearest tenth, it is the same number. [Rounding]

9. C Round $1858.46 to $2000, $201.36 to 200, $109.32 to $100, $27.54 to $30, $22.11 to $20.00, and $34.17 to $30.00. Add the rounded numbers

10. G Round 147 square feet to 150. Then divide 150 ÷ 10 (the number of square feet covered by one bag) = 15 bags needed. [Estimation]

11. C Round $159.95 to $160. Multiply 160 × 0.25 = 40. Subtract 160 − 40 to get the sale price of a bicycle: $120. [Estimation]

Performance Assessment Applied Math (pages 104–115)

A. C The sequence is made up of odd numbers 3, 5, 7, 9, 11

1. D 6 × 3 = 18; 18 × 2 = 36; 36 × 2 = 72; 72 × 2 = 144; 144 × 2 = 288. You will never get 96. [Functions and Patterns]

2. H (2 quarters = $0.50) + (3 dimes = $0.30) + (3 nickels = $0.15) + (6 pennies = $0.06) = $1.01. [Money]

3. B This number is 403. [Recognize numbers]

4. J 20 + 5 = 25 [Equations]

5. C $40,000 was taken in at the Giants–Brewers game and $20,000 was taken in at the Braves–Marlins Game. $40,000 is two times $20,000. [Graphs]

6. H If you know the number of students each row can seat, you can multiply that by the number of rows to find the number of students the gym can seat. [Pre-Solution]

7. B First multiply $350 × 0.06 = $21. Then add $350 + $21 = $371.00 for the new price. [Percents in Context]

8. H The dahlia is 24 inches tall. [Charts]

9. A Add $235.04 + $117.52 + $29.38 = $381.94 [Decimals in context]

10. F As a decimal, 1% is the same as 0.01 [Percents in Context]

11. D The total of state income tax each month ($37.29) is multiplied by the number of months in a year (12) [Equations]

12. H Round his income to $2000 and his total deductions to $400. His net monthly income is found by $2000 − $400 = $1600. [Rounding]

13. B Divide 3 ÷ 2 = $1\frac{1}{2}$. 1 inch = $1\frac{1}{2}$ feet. [Ratio and Proportion]

14. F 36 inches = 3 feet. This is $1\frac{1}{2}$ times as high as the original chest. Multiply the length of 3 feet × $1\frac{1}{2}$ = $4\frac{1}{2}$ feet, which is equal to 54 inches. Multiply the width of 2 feet × $1\frac{1}{2}$ = 3 feet, which is equal to 36 inches. [Ratio and Proportion]

15. D Multiply. 3 × $12.95 = $38.85. Then multiply $38.85 × 0.06 = $2.33 tax. The total cost of the paneling is $38.85 + $2.33 = $41.18. [Percents in Context]

16. H To find the surface area: For the top and bottom: $2 \times (3 \times 2) = 12$. Next find the front and back: $2 \times (3 \times 2) = 12$. Then to find the left and right sides: $2 \times (2 \times 2) = 8$. Last add $12 + 12 + 8 = 32$ ft^2. [Surface Area]

17. A There are 4 computer terminals. This is multiplied by 7 minutes: $4 \times 7 = 28$ minutes. This is about $\frac{1}{2}$ hour. [Estimation]

18. H Circumference is used to find the distance around the outside of a circle [Parts of a Circle]

19. B $\frac{1}{2}$ is the largest fraction [Comparison]

20. J This is a right triangle [Triangles]

21. B There are 9 sections. If 3 of the sections are devoted to native animals, this is $\frac{1}{3}$ of the sections. [Fractional part]

22. G $1 \times 2 \times 5 = 10$ [Missing Element]

23. A 0.910 is greater than 0.905 and less than 0.916. [Comparison]

24. J $11 \times 2 = 22$; $22 - 5 = 17$ [Functions and Patterns]

25. B This five-sided figure is a pentagon. [Plane Figures]

26. F The distance around Stone Memorial is 3.6 miles. The distance Pine Meadow is 4.8 miles. $\frac{3.6}{4.8} = \frac{3}{4}$. [Fractional Part]

27. B Divide $4.2 \div 0.62 = 6.77$ kilometers [Decimals in Context]

28. G 4.8 is equal to $4\frac{8}{10}$. [Equivalent Form]

29. D Each mile takes 40 minutes to hike. It is 3.6 miles around Russian Bear. $3.6 \times 40 = 2.4$ hours. $144 \div 60 = 2.4$, which is 2 hours 24 minutes. That is almost 2 hours 25 minutes. [Time]

30. F Similar figures are the same shape but can differ in size. [Similarity]

31. A 129,612 is rounded to 130,000 when rounded to the nearest thousand. [Rounding]

32. J 8.973 is rounded to 9 when rounded to the nearest whole number and to the nearest tenth. [Rounding]

33. B 3 feet is equal to one yard, which is close to one meter. [Length]

34. F The perimeter is found by $58 + 52 + 45 + 40 = 195$ feet. [Perimeter]

35. D First divide $6 \div 2 = 3$. Then multiply $3 \times \$8.75 = \$26.25$. [Decimals in Context]

36. H This sidewalk is 45 feet in length. $45 \div 5 = 9$ sections. [Whole numbers in Context]

37. C Interest expense is 4% of all expenses. 4% of $100,000 can be found by multiplying $100,000 \times 0.04 = \$4000$. [Percents in Context]

38. H The interest expense can be found by using the equation $E = $ (total expenses for one week) $\times 52 \times 0.04$. [Equations]

39. A Add $22.2\% + 4\% + 9.1\% = 35.3\%$. [Percents in Context]

40. H Multiply $70,000 by 0.3 to find the amount of the reduction, $21,000. Subtract $\$70,000 - \$21,000 = \$49,000$.

41. B The temperature in Chicago increased by 11° between April and May. This was the largest increase of any city. [Graphs]

42. F New York and Chicago both had temperatures below 65° in four of the five months. [Graphs]

43. D The cities in order from least to greatest average temperatures in May are Chicago, New York, Los Angeles, Atlanta, and Houston. [Graphs]

44. H First add the temperatures in March: $40° + 50° + 70° + 74° + 65° = 299$. Then divide $299 \div 5 = 59$ with a remainder of 4. This is rounded to 60°. [Estimation]

45. D $\frac{15}{30} = \frac{1}{2}$ inch [Fractional Part]

46. H Divide $120 \div 30 = 4$ inches. [Reasonableness of answer]

47. B Multiply $\$1.89 \times 10 = \$18.90$. [Money]

48. F First find $\frac{1}{3}$ of 300 miles by $300 \times \frac{1}{3} = 100$ miles. They still have 200 miles to travel $(300 - 100)$. Then divide $200 \div 4 = 50$ miles per hour. [Fractions in Context]

49. A On the original map, 240 miles would be 8 inches $(240 \div 30)$. Using a scale of 1 inch = 40 miles, 240 miles would be 6 inches on the map $(240 \div 40)$. [Estimation]

50. G The pattern is $+2, -1$. The next figure in the pattern will have 3 sections. [Patterns and Shapes]